W9-AUX-017

WITHDRAWN

SIZZLING 100 RED HOT AND
FIERY CHILLI DISHES
CHILLIES

SIZZLING

100 RED HOT AND FIERY CHILLI DISHES

CHILLIES

MORE THAN 100 SCORCHING RECIPES FROM AROUND THE
WORLD, SHOWN IN OVER 400 STEP-BY-STEP PHOTOGRAPHS

JENNI FLEETWOOD

southwater

This edition is published by Southwater, an imprint of Anness Publishing Ltd, Hermes House,
88–89 Blackfriars Road, London SE1 8HA; tel. 020 7401 2077; fax 020 7633 9499

www.southwaterbooks.com; www.annesspublishing.com

If you like the images in this book and would like to investigate using them for publishing, promotions
or advertising, please visit our website www.practicalpictures.com for more information.

UK distributor: Book Trade Services; tel. 0116 2759086;
fax 0116 2759090; uksales@booktradeservices.com;
exportsales@booktradeservices.com
North American distributor: National Book Network;
tel. 301 459 3366; fax 301 429 5746; www.nbnbooks.com
Australian distributor: Pan Macmillan Australia;
tel. 1300 135 113; fax 1300 135 103;
customer.service@macmillan.com.au
New Zealand distributor: David Bateman Ltd;
tel. (09) 415 7664; fax (09) 415 8892

Publisher: Joanna Lorenz
Managing Editor: Linda Fraser
Project Editors: Jennifer Schofield and Laura Seber
Recipes contributed by: Catherine Atkinson, Alex Barker, Angela Boggiano, Carla Capalbo,
Kit Chan, Maxine Clark, Jacqueline Clarke, Trish Davies, Patrizia Diemling, Matthew Drennan, Tessa Evelegh,
Silvana Franco, Shirley Gill, Brian Glover, Rosamund Grant, Nicola Graimes, Deh-Ta Hsuing, Shehzad Husain,
Christine Ingram, Manisha Kanani, Lucy Knox, Lesley Mackley, Sally Mansfield, Norma Miller, Jane Milton,
Sallie Morris, Annie Nichols, Jennie Shapter, Liz Trigg, Laura Washburn and Jeni Wright
Photography: Karl Adamson, Edward Allwright, Nicki Dowey, James Duncan, Ian Garlick, Michelle Garrett,
Amanda Heywood, Ferguson Hill, Janine Hosegood, David Jordan, Dave King, William Lingwood,
Patrick McLeavey, Steve Moss, Thomas Odulate, Craig Robertson, Simon Smith and Sam Stowell
Designer: Nigel Partridge
Production Controller: Mai-Ling Collyer

ETHICAL TRADING POLICY

Because of our ongoing ecological investment programme, you, as our customer, can have the pleasure and
reassurance of knowing that a tree is being cultivated on your behalf to naturally replace the materials used to
make the book you are holding. For further information about this scheme, go to www.annesspublishing.com/trees

A CIP catalogue record for this book is available from the British Library.

Previously published as part of a larger volume, *The Chilli-Lover's Cookbook*

NOTES

Bracketed terms are intended for American readers.
For all recipes, quantities are given in both metric and imperial measures and, where appropriate, in standard cups and spoons.
Follow one set of measures, but not a mixture, because they are not interchangeable.
Standard spoon and cup measures are level. 1 tsp = 5ml, 1 tbsp = 15ml, 1 cup = 250ml/8fl oz.
Australian standard tablespoons are 20ml. Australian readers should use 3 tsp in place of 1 tbsp for measuring small quantities.
American pints are 16fl oz/2 cups. American readers should use 20fl oz/2.5 cups in place of 1 pint when measuring liquids.
Electric oven temperatures in this book are for conventional ovens. When using a fan oven, the temperature may need to be
reduced by about 10–20°C/20–40°F. Since ovens vary, you should check with your manufacturer's instruction book for guidance.
Medium (US large) eggs are used unless otherwise stated.

PUBLISHER'S NOTE

CONTENTS

INTRODUCTION

Of all the ingredients available to the enthusiastic cook, chillies are perhaps the most challenging. They can transform the simplest dish into a taste sensation, providing a whole range of special effects, from the tantalizing tingle on the tongue to an explosion of fiery flavour.

These powerful pods originated in South America, but now form a very important part of many of the world's major cuisines. India is the largest producer and exporter of chillies, with much of the crop going for local consumption. Thailand, Japan, Turkey, Nigeria, Ethiopia, Uganda, Kenya and Tanzania are also prime producers, exporting chillies to other countries around the globe. The country most closely associated with chillies, however, is Mexico. A mecca for chilli-lovers, every region has its own varieties. Chillies are valued not merely for their heat, but for their flavour, and accomplished Mexican cooks will often use several different types in a single dish, in order to obtain a precise taste.

Fortunately for those of us who like to have some warning as to whether the contents of our shopping basket will be fragrant or fiery, there are several rating systems for the heat in chillies. Possibly the best known of these grades chillies in Scoville units, but these are somewhat unwieldy, being measured in thousands, and a simpler system, grading chillies out of ten, is more often used today. The hottest chilli is generally held to be the habanero, with a heat scale rating of 10, while mild bell peppers register zero.

What makes one chilli hotter than another is the amount of capsaicin each contains. This chemical, largely located in the fibrous placenta and seeds, is a powerful irritant, which is why chillies must always be handled with care. As compensation for this inconvenience, capsaicin stimulates the brain to produce hormones called endorphins, so these sizzling stars of the culinary stage not only taste great, but make us feel good, too.

Below: The long green anaheim chilli

THE CHILLI FAMILY

There are more than two hundred different types of chilli, but only a few of the most popular varieties – like serranos, jalapeños and cayennes – make it on to supermarket shelves. Even then, they are often unimaginatively described. A label that merely reads "red chillies" or even "hot red chillies" is not very helpful, so the onus is on all of us who love good food to learn how to identify the various varieties.

How do you know whether a chilli is hot or not? Are small chillies hotter than big ones? Are red chillies hotter than green? The answer to the last two questions is no. Although some of the world's hottest chillies are tiny, there are a few large varieties that are real scorchers. Colour isn't an infallible indicator either. Most chillies start out green and ripen to red, but some start yellow and ripen to red, and yet others start yellow and stay yellow, and across the spectrum you'll find hot varieties. To confuse the issue still further, chillies on the same plant can have different degrees of heat, and in at least one type of chilli, the top of the fruit is hotter than the bottom.

The best way to familiarize yourself with chillies is to try as many varieties as possible. This means growing your own or finding a good supplier, either via the Internet or by chatting to other *chilliheads*, as aficionados are commonly known. Chilli seeds are

Left: Chillies come in various shapes, sizes, colours, and strengths, and can be bought fresh or dried.

available by mail order, as are fresh and dried chillies. The latter travel well, can be stored like other spices, and are delicious when rehydrated.

In the descriptions that follow, chillies are listed by heat, with 10 being the hottest.

Below: Ancho chillies

Ancho

Heat scale 3: Dried poblanos, these are larger than most other dried chillies. Open the packet and savour the wonderful fruity aroma – similar to dates or dried figs. Like poblanos, anchos can be stuffed but also taste great in stir-fries.

Anaheim

Heat scale 2–3: About 15cm/6in long and 5cm/2in wide, these chillies are good candidates for roasting and stuffing. The flavour is fresh and fruity, like a cross between tart apples and green bell peppers.

Guajillo

Heat scale 3: These dried chillies are about 15cm/6in long, with rough skin. They have a mild, slightly bitter flavour, suggestive of green tea. Guajillos are used in many classic salsas.

Italia

Heat scale 3: Juicy and refreshing, these dark green chillies ripen to a rich, dark red. They taste great sliced into salads and have an affinity for tropical fruit, especially mangoes.

Mulato

Heat scale 3: A dried chilli with a thin, wrinkled, dark brown skin, this is related to the ancho. The flavour is smoky and herby.

Poblano

Heat scale 3: Big and beautiful, poblanos look like sweet bell peppers, and are perfect for stuffing. The flavour bears a passing resemblance to that of bell pepper, but is spicier, with peachy overtones. See also Ancho.

Pasado

Heat scale 3–4: Very dark brown in colour, these skinny, dried chillies are generally about 10cm/4in long. When rehydrated, they taste lemony, with a hint of cucumber and apple.

Cascabel

Heat scale 4: The name translates as "little rattle", and refers to the sound the seeds make inside these round dried chillies. The woody, nutty flavour is best appreciated when the skin is removed. Soak them, then either scrape the flesh off the skin (as when eating a whole kiwi fruit) or press it through a sieve.

Cherry Hot

Heat scale 4: Pungent, with thick walls, these sweet chillies look like large versions of the fruit for which they are named. The skins can be tough, so they are best peeled.

Above: Cherry hot chillies have a sweetish flavour and make good pickles.

Preparing Fresh Chillies

As many cooks have found to their cost, the capsaicin in chillies is a powerful irritant, especially to sensitive areas like the eyes, nose and mouth. Wear gloves or wash your hands well in hot soapy water after handling chillies.

Using a sharp knife, cut each chilli in half lengthwise. Trim the stalk end from both halves. Scrape out the seeds and membrane. Finely chop or slice the chillies. If preferred, the seeds can be left in. This will give a hotter result.

Costeno Amarillo

Heat scale 4: Not to be confused with the much hotter Aji Amarillo, this is a pale orange dried chilli, which is ideal for use in yellow salsas and Mexican *moles*. It has a citrus flavour and is often used to give depth to soups.

Pasilla

Heat scale 4: Quite large and about 15cm/6in in length, pasillas are dried chilaca chillies. Their fruity, liquorice flavour works well with seafood, *mole* sauce and mushrooms.

Fresno

Heat scale 5: Plump and cylindrical, with tapered ends, these fresh chillies are most often sold red, although you will sometimes find green or yellow ones in the shops. They resemble jalapeños in appearance, and can be substituted for them.

Jalapeño

Heat scale 4–7: Green and red jalapeños are frequently seen in our supermarkets. Plump and stubby, like fat fingers, they have shiny skins. The flavour is piquant, almost grassy, and they are widely used in salsas, salads, dips and stews.

Hungarian Wax Chillies

Heat scale 5: These really do look waxy, like novelty candles. Unlike many chillies, they start off yellow, not green. It is not necessary to peel them, and they are often used in salads and salsas.

Preparing Dried Chillies

1 Wipe off surface dirt from the chillies. Soak in hot water to cover for 20–30 minutes until softened.

2 Drain, cut off any stalks, then slit the chillies and scrape out the seeds. Slice or chop. For a purée, process with a little of the soaking water. Sieve if necessary.

Left: Jalapeño chillies are the most commonly used chillies in Mexican food.

Aji Amarillo

Heat scale 6–7: There are several varieties, including one that is yellow when fully ripe, and a large brown aji that is frequently dried. The chillies average about 10cm/4in in length and look rather like miniature windsocks.

Cayenne

Heat scale 6–8: These popular chillies range from 7.5cm/3in to 17cm/6½in in length, and have a sweet yet fiery flavour. The basis of cayenne pepper, they are also used in sauces.

Above: One of the several varieties of Cayenne chilli.

Chipotle

Heat scale 6–10: Smoke-dried jalapeños, these have wrinkled, dark red skin and thick flesh. Chipotles need long, slow cooking to soften them and bring out their intriguing smoky flavour.

Serrano

Heat scale 7: Usually sold green, Serranos are about 4cm/1½in long and slender. An important ingredient in guacamole, the flavour is clean and crisp, with a suggestion of citrus.

Bird's Eye

Heat scale 8: Very small and extremely hot, these come from a highly volatile family of chillies that are found in Africa, Asia, the United States and the Caribbean, and often labelled simply as "Thai chillies".

De Arbol

Heat scale 8: More often sold dried than fresh, these smooth cayenne-type chillies are slim and curvaceous. A warm orange red colour, these chillies combine blistering heat with a clean, grassy flavour.

Manzano

Heat scale 9: This delicious chilli is very hot and fruity. About the size of a crab apple, it is the only variety of chilli to have purple/black seeds.

Habanero

Heat scale 10: These lantern-shaped chillies have a wonderful, fruity flavour, and a surprisingly delicate aroma, but they are ultra hot, so handle them with extreme care. Always wear strong gloves, and don't stand over a food processor when blending them, or the fumes may burn your face.

Scotch Bonnets

Heat scale 10: Often confused with habanero chillies, which they closely resemble. Scotch bonnets are grown in Jamaica and are the main ingredient of jerk seasoning.

Above: A dried form of the explosively hot bird's eye chilli.

CHILLI PRODUCTS

The universal passion for chillies has spawned a huge industry in chilli products. Here are some hot favourites:

Chilli Powders

Anyone buying chilli powder could be forgiven for expecting the jar to contain powdered chilli, but this product is in fact a blend of several ingredients, designed specifically for making chilli con carne. In addition to ground hot chillies, it tends to include cumin, oregano, salt and garlic powder.
Pure powders – the whole chilli and nothing but the chilli – are less easy to come by, but are available from specialist shops and by mail order. Ancho, caribe and New Mexico red powders are relatively mild (heat scale 3). Pasilla, a rich, dark powder, registers 4 on the heat scale, while chipotle is a little hotter.

*Above:
Red and
green tabasco
sauce*

Cayenne pepper is a very fine ground powder from the capsicum frutescens variety of chilli. The placenta and seeds are included, so it is very hot.
Paprika is a fine, rich red powder made from mild chillies. The core and seeds are removed, but the flavour can still be quite pungent. Look out for *pimentón dulce*, a delicious smoked paprika from Estramadura in Spain.

*Right: Crushed
chilli flakes*

Crushed Chillies

Dried chilli flakes are widely available. Sprinkle them on pizzas or add to cooked dishes for a last-minute lift. Crushed dried green jalapeño chillies are a useful storecupboard item, combining considerable heat with a delicious sweetness.

Chilli Pastes

One of the world's most famous chilli pastes – harissa – comes from North Africa. A spicy blend of red chillies, coriander and cumin, it can be served solo or with puréed tomatoes as a side dish for dipping pieces of barbecued meat. A little harissa is wonderful added to soups and stews.
A hot chilli paste is easy to make at home. Simply seed fresh chillies, then purée them in a food processor until smooth. Store small amounts in the refrigerator for up to 1 week, or freeze for up to 6 months.

Chilli Sauces

The world's most famous chilli sauce is Tabasco, developed in Louisiana by E McIlhenny in the latter half of the 19th century. Chillies are matured in oak barrels to develop the sauce's unique flavour. Try mixing a few drops with fresh lime juice as a baste next time you grill (broil) salmon steaks, or add to sauces, soups or casseroles. Also available is Tabasco Jalapeño Sauce – often referred to as green Tabasco sauce. Milder in flavour than the red version, it is good with nachos, hamburgers or on pizza.

Chilli sauces are also widely used in Asia. Chinese chilli sauce is quite hot and spicy, with a hint of fruitiness thanks to the inclusion of apples or plums. For a milder flavour, look out for sweet chilli sauce, which is a blend of red chillies, sugar and tamarind juice from Sichuan. Vietnamese chilli sauce is very hot, while the Thai sauce tends to be thicker and spicier. Bottled chilli sauces are used both for cooking and as a dip.

Chilli Oils

These have a pleasant smell, and a concentrated flavour, much stronger than chilli sauce, and should be used sparingly. Toss them with pasta, add a dash to a stir-fry, or drizzle them over pizzas. In China and South-east Asia, chilli oil is a popular dipping sauce. Two types are widely sold. The first is a simple infusion of dried chillies, onions, garlic and salt in vegetable oil. The second, XO chilli oil, is flavoured with dried scallops.

Convenient Chillies
Jars of whole chillies in white wine vinegar are handy for the home cook. Also look out for minced (ground) chillies. After opening, jars must be tightly closed, kept in the refrigerator and the contents consumed by the use-by date.

The great thing about dips and relishes

is that the diner is in the hot seat and can

add as much fire as he or she requires. For sizzling

effect, spoon on Green Fire or Demon Salsa.

Adding a milder ingredient, as in Avocado and

Sweet Pepper Salsa, will damp down the flames,

while Spicy Sweetcorn relish has

warmth without wallop.

Dips and Relishes

GREEN FIRE

ALSO KNOWN AS SALSA VERDE, THIS IS A CLASSIC GREEN SALSA IN WHICH CAPERS PLAY AN IMPORTANT PART. MAKE IT WITH GREEN CAYENNE CHILLIES OR THE MILDER JALAPEÑOS.

SERVES FOUR

INGREDIENTS
  2–4 fresh green chillies
  8 spring onions (scallions)
  2 garlic cloves
  50g/2oz/½ cup salted capers
  1 fresh tarragon sprig
  bunch of fresh parsley
  grated (shredded) rind and juice
   of 1 lime
  juice of 1 lemon
  90ml/6 tbsp olive oil
  15ml/1 tbsp green Tabasco sauce
  ground black pepper

1 Cut the chillies in half and scrape out and discard the seeds. Trim the spring onions and cut them into short lengths. Cut the garlic in half. Mix in a food processor and pulse until chopped.

2 Use your fingertips to rub the excess salt off the capers but do not rinse them (see Cook's Tip). Add the capers, tarragon and parsley to the food processor and pulse again until they are quite finely chopped.

3 Transfer the mixture to a small bowl. Stir in the lime rind and juice, lemon juice and olive oil. Stir lightly so the citrus juice and oil do not emulsify.

4 Add green Tabasco and black pepper to taste. Chill until ready to serve but do not prepare more than 8 hours in advance.

COOK'S TIP
If you can only find capers pickled in vinegar, they must be rinsed well in cold water before using.

AVOCADO AND SWEET RED PEPPER SALSA

THIS SIMPLE SALSA IS A FIRE-AND-ICE MIXTURE THAT COMBINES HOT CHILLI WITH COOLING AVOCADO. SERVE IT WITH CORN CHIPS FOR DIPPING.

SERVES FOUR

INGREDIENTS
  2 ripe avocados
  1 red onion
  1 sweet red (bell) pepper
  4 fresh green chillies
  30ml/2 tbsp chopped fresh
   coriander (cilantro)
  30ml/2 tbsp sunflower oil
  juice of 1 lemon
  salt and ground black pepper

1 Cut the avocados in half and remove the stone (pit) from each. Scoop out the flesh and dice it. Finely chop the red onion.

2 Slice the top off the sweet red pepper and pull out the central core. Shake out any remaining seeds. Cut the pepper into thin strips, then into dice.

3 Cut the chillies in half lengthways, scrape out and discard the seeds and finely chop the flesh. Put it in a jug (pitcher) and mix in the coriander, oil, lemon juice and salt and pepper to taste.

4 Place the avocado, red onion and pepper in a bowl. Pour in the chilli dressing and toss well. Serve immediately.

COOK'S TIP
Serrano chillies would be a good choice, or moderate them with the milder Anaheim if you like.

CHILLI AND PESTO SALSA

USE LONG SLIM RED CHILLIES TO MAKE THIS AROMATIC SALSA, WHICH IS DELICIOUS OVER FISH AND CHICKEN. IT IS ALSO GOOD TOSSED WITH PASTA RIBBONS OR USED TO DRESS A FRESH AVOCADO AND TOMATO SALAD. YOU CAN MAKE IT INTO A DIP BY MIXING IT WITH A LITTLE MAYONNAISE OR SOUR CREAM.

SERVES FOUR

INGREDIENTS
   50g/2oz/1⅓ cups fresh coriander
     (cilantro) leaves
   15g/½oz/¼ cup fresh parsley
   2 fresh red chillies
   1 garlic clove, halved
   50g/2oz/½ cup shelled pistachio nuts
   25g/1oz/⅓ cup freshly grated
     (shredded) Parmesan cheese
   90ml/6 tbsp olive oil
   juice of 2 limes
   salt and ground black pepper

1 Process the coriander and parsley in a food processor until finely chopped. Cut the chillies in half, scrape out and discard seeds. Add to the herbs, with the garlic and process until finely chopped.

2 Add the pistachio nuts to the herb mixture and pulse until they are roughly chopped. Scrape the mixture into a bowl and stir in the Parmesan cheese, olive oil and lime juice.

3 Add salt and pepper to taste. Spoon the mixture into a serving bowl, cover and chill until ready to serve.

FIERY CITRUS SALSA

THIS VERY UNUSUAL SALSA, WHICH COMBINES FRUIT WITH CHILLIES, MAKES A FANTASTIC MARINADE FOR SHELLFISH AND IT IS ALSO DELICIOUS DRIZZLED OVER BARBECUE-COOKED MEAT.

SERVES FOUR

INGREDIENTS
   1 orange
   1 green apple
   2 fresh red chillies
   1 garlic clove
   8 fresh mint leaves
   juice of 1 lemon
   salt and ground black pepper

1 Slice the base off the orange so that it will stand firmly on a chopping board. Using a sharp knife, remove the peel and pith in sections.

2 Holding the orange over a bowl to catch the juices, cut away the segments from the membrane, letting them fall into the bowl. Squeeze any juice from the remaining membrane into the bowl.

3 Peel, quarter and core the apple. Put it in a food processor. Cut the chillies in half and scrape out and discard the seeds. Add them to the food processor with the orange segments and juice, garlic and fresh mint.

4 Process until smooth. Then, with the motor running, pour in the lemon juice through the feeder tube. Season to taste. Pour into a bowl and serve immediately.

VARIATION
If you're feeling really daring, don't seed the chillies! They will make the salsa particularly hot and fierce.

DEMON SALSA

THIS IS A SCORCHINGLY HOT SALSA MADE WITH TWO TYPES OF CHILLIES, AND SHOULD BE TREATED WITH THE UTMOST CAUTION. SPREAD IT SPARINGLY ON COOKED MEATS AND BURGERS.

3 Use a clean dishtowel to rub the skins off the blistered chillies.

4 Try not to touch the chillies with your bare hands: use a fork to hold them and slice them open with a sharp knife. Scrape out and discard the seeds, then finely chop the flesh.

5 Cut the jalapeño chillies in half lengthways, remove the seeds, then finely slice them into tiny strips. Mix both types of chilli, the tomatoes and the chopped parsley in a bowl.

SERVES FOUR TO SIX

INGREDIENTS
    6 fresh habanero chillies or
      Scotch bonnets
    2 ripe tomatoes
    4 fresh green jalapeño chillies
    30ml/2 tbsp chopped fresh parsley
    30ml/2 tbsp olive oil
    15ml/1 tbsp balsamic or
      sherry vinegar
    salt

1 Skewer a habanero or Scotch bonnet chilli on a metal fork and hold it in a gas flame for 2–3 minutes, turning until the skin darkens and blisters. Repeat with the remaining chillies. Set aside.

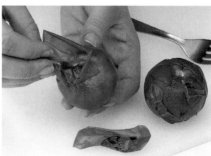

2 Skewer the tomatoes one at a time and hold in a gas flame for 1–2 minutes, until the skin splits and wrinkles. Slip off the skins, halve the tomatoes, then use a teaspoon to scoop out and discard the seeds. Chop the flesh very finely.

6 Make a dressing by mixing the olive oil and vinegar with a little salt, pour this over the salsa and toss to mix. Cover the bowl. Chill for up to 3 days.

ROASTED TOMATO SALSA

Slow roasting these tomatoes to a semi-dried state results in a very rich, full-flavoured sweet sauce. The costeno amarillo chilli is mild and has a fresh light flavour, making it the perfect partner for the rich tomato taste.

SERVES SIX

INGREDIENTS
500g/1¼ lb tomatoes
8 small shallots
5 garlic cloves
1 fresh rosemary sprig
2 dried costeno amarillo chillies
grated (shredded) rind and juice of
½ small lemon
30ml/2 tbsp extra virgin olive oil
1.5ml/¼ tsp soft dark brown sugar
sea salt

1 Preheat the oven to 160°C/325°F/ Gas 3. Cut the tomatoes into quarters and place them on a baking tray.

2 Peel the shallots and garlic cloves, and add them to the baking tray. Sprinkle with sea salt. Roast in the oven for 1¼ hours or until the tomatoes are beginning to dry. Do not let them burn or they will have a bitter taste.

3 Leave the tomatoes to cool, then peel off the skins and chop the flesh finely. Place in a bowl. Remove the tough outer layer of skin from any shallots.

4 Using a large, sharp knife, chop the shallots and garlic roughly, place them with the tomatoes in a bowl and mix.

5 Strip the rosemary leaves from the woody stem and chop them finely. Add half to the tomato and shallot mixture and mix lightly.

COOK'S TIP
This salsa is great with tuna or sea bass and makes a marvellous sandwich filling when teamed with creamy cheese.

6 Soak the chillies in hot water for about 10 minutes until soft. Drain, remove the stalks, slit them and scrape out the seeds with a sharp knife. Chop the chilli flesh finely and add it to the tomato mixture.

7 Stir in the lemon rind and juice, the olive oil and the sugar. Mix well, taste and add more salt if needed. Cover and chill for at least 1 hour before serving, sprinkled with the remaining rosemary. It will keep for 1 week, refrigerated.

MANGO AND CHILLI SALSA

THIS HAS A FRESH, FRUITY TASTE AND IS PERFECT WITH FISH OR AS A CONTRAST TO RICH, CREAMY DISHES. THE BRIGHT COLOURS MAKE IT AN ATTRACTIVE ADDITION TO ANY TABLE.

SERVES FOUR

INGREDIENTS
  2 fresh red fresno chillies
  2 ripe mangoes
  ½ white onion
  small bunch of fresh
    coriander (cilantro)
  grated (shredded) rind and juice
    of 1 lime

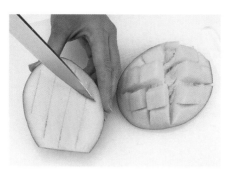

1 To peel the chillies, spear them on a long-handled metal skewer and roast them over the flame of a gas burner, turning the chillies continually, until the skins blister and darken. Do not let the flesh burn. Alternatively, dry-fry them in a frying pan until the skins are scorched.

2 Place the roasted chillies in a strong plastic bag and tie the top. Set aside.

VARIATION
For a refreshing change, look out for juicy Italia chillies, which have a wonderful affinity for mangoes.

3 Meanwhile, put one of the mangoes on a board and cut off a thick slice close to the flat side of the stone (pit). Turn the mango round and repeat on the other side. Score the flesh on each thick slice with criss-cross lines at 1cm/½in intervals, taking care not to cut through the skin. Repeat with the second mango.

4 Fold the mango halves inside out so that the mango flesh stands proud of the skin, in neat dice. Carefully slice these off the skin and into a bowl. Cut off the flesh adhering to each stone, dice it and add it to the bowl.

5 Remove the roasted chillies from the bag and carefully peel off the skins. Cut off the stalks, then slit the chillies and scrape out the seeds with a sharp knife. Discard the seeds.

6 Chop the white onion and the coriander finely and add them to the diced mango. Chop the chilli flesh finely and add it to the mixture in the bowl, together with the lime rind and juice. Toss the ingredients in the bowl thoroughly, then cover and chill for at least 1 hour before serving. The salsa will keep for 2–3 days in the refrigerator.

ROASTED SERRANO AND TOMATO SALSA

ROASTING THE CHILLIES GIVES A GREATER DEPTH TO THE TASTE OF THIS SALSA, WHICH ALSO BENEFITS FROM THE ROUNDED FLAVOUR OF ROASTED TOMATOES.

SERVES SIX

INGREDIENTS
  500g/1¼lb tomatoes
  2 fresh serrano chillies
  1 onion
  juice of 1 lime
  large bunch of fresh
    coriander (cilantro)
  salt

1 Preheat the oven to 200°C/400°F/ Gas 6. Cut the tomatoes into quarters and place them in a roasting pan. Add the chillies. Roast for 45–60 minutes, until charred and softened.

2 Place the roasted chillies in a strong plastic bag. Tie the top to keep the steam in and set aside for 20 minutes. Leave the tomatoes to cool slightly, then remove the skins and dice the flesh.

3 Chop the onion finely, then place in a bowl and add the lime juice and the diced tomatoes.

4 Remove the chillies from the bag and peel off the skins. Cut off the stalks, then slit the chillies and scrape out the seeds with a sharp knife. Chop the chillies roughly and add them to the onion mixture. Mix well.

5 Chop the coriander and add most to the salsa. Add salt, cover and chill for at least 1 hour before serving, sprinkled with the remaining coriander. This salsa will keep in the refrigerator for 1 week.

CHUNKY CHERRY CHILLI AND TOMATO SALSA

PUNGENT CHERRY CHILLIES AND SWEET CHERRY TOMATOES ARE MIXED WITH COOLING CUCUMBER IN THIS DELICIOUS DILL-SEASONED SALSA.

SERVES FOUR

INGREDIENTS
    1 ridge cucumber
    5ml/1 tsp sea salt
    500g/1¼lb cherry tomatoes
    1–2 fresh hot cherry chillies
    1 lemon
    1 garlic clove, crushed
    45ml/3 tbsp chilli oil
    30ml/2 tbsp chopped fresh dill
    salt and ground black pepper

1 Trim the ends off the cucumber and cut it into 2.5cm/1in lengths, then cut each piece lengthways into thin slices.

2 Spread out the cucumber slices in a colander and sprinkle them with the sea salt. Leave for 5 minutes until the cucumber has wilted.

COOK'S TIPS
• Cherry chillies are usually only moderately hot, but have quite a pungent, biting flavour. One could easily be sufficient to flavour the salsa.
• If you do not have gas roast the chillies under a hot grill (broiler) until blistered and blackened.

3 Wash the cucumber slices well under cold water and pat them dry with kitchen paper.

4 Quarter the cherry tomatoes and place in a bowl with the wilted cucumber. Skewer the chilli (or chillies) on a metal fork and hold in a gas flame for 2–3 minutes, turning often, until blistered and blackened. Slit, scrape out the seeds, then finely chop the flesh. Add it to the bowl.

5 Grate the lemon rind finely and place in a small bowl. Squeeze the lemon and add the juice to the bowl, with the garlic, chilli oil and dill. Add salt and pepper to taste, and whisk the ingredients together with a fork.

6 Pour the chilli oil dressing over the tomato and cucumber and toss well. Leave the salsa to marinate at room temperature for at least 2–3 hours before serving.

BLACK BEAN SALSA

THIS SALSA HAS A VERY STRIKING APPEARANCE. IT IS RARE TO FIND A BLACK SPICE AND IT PROVIDES A WONDERFUL CONTRAST TO THE MORE COMMON REDS AND GREENS ON THE PLATE.

SERVES FOUR

INGREDIENTS

130g/4½oz/generous ½ cup black
  beans, soaked overnight in water
1 pasado chilli
2 fresh red fresno chillies
1 red onion
grated (shredded) rind and juice
  of 1 lime
30ml/2 tbsp Mexican beer (optional)
15ml/1 tbsp olive oil
small bunch of fresh coriander
  (cilantro), chopped
salt

1 Drain the beans, rinse them thoroughly and put them in a large pan. Pour in water to cover. Do not add salt as this toughens the outside skin and prevents the bean from cooking properly. Place the lid on the pan and bring to the boil. Lower the heat slightly and simmer the beans for about 40 minutes or until tender. They should still have a little bite and should not have begun to disintegrate. Drain, rinse under cold water, then drain again and leave the beans until cold.

2 Soak the pasado chilli in hot water for about 20 minutes until softened. Drain, remove the stalk, then slit the chilli and, using a small sharp knife, scrape out the seeds and discard them. Chop the flesh finely.

COOK'S TIP
Pasado chillies are always sold in their dried, roasted form. Dark, almost black, in colour, they have a subtle citrus flavour and are only mildly hot.

3 Spear the fresno chillies on a long-handled metal skewer and roast them over the flame of a gas burner, turning the chillies all the time, until the skins blister and darken. Do not let the flesh burn. Alternatively, dry-fry them in a griddle pan until the skins are scorched.

4 Place the roasted chillies in a strong plastic bag and tie the top to keep the steam in. Set aside for 20 minutes.

5 Meanwhile, chop the red onion finely. Remove the chillies from the bag and peel off the skins. Slit them, remove and discard the seeds, and chop them finely.

6 Tip the beans into a bowl and add the onion and both types of chilli. Stir in the lime rind and juice, and beer, if using, then add the oil and coriander. Season with salt and mix well. Leave the salsa for a day or two to allow the flavours to develop fully. Serve chilled.

SPICY TOMATO AND CHILLI DIP

GET YOUR TASTE BUDS TINGLING WITH THIS TANGY DIP, SPIKED WITH FRESH GREEN CHILLIES. IT IS DELICIOUS SERVED WITH DEEP-FRIED POTATO SKINS OR HASH BROWNS.

SERVES FOUR

INGREDIENTS
   1 shallot, halved
   2 garlic cloves, halved
   handful of fresh basil leaves, plus
     extra, to garnish
   500g/1¼lb ripe tomatoes
   30ml/2 tbsp olive oil
   2 fresh green chillies
   salt and ground black pepper

COOK'S TIP
Use green serrano or jalapeño chillies. Anaheims are also suitable, and will give a milder result.

1 Place the shallot and garlic in a blender or food processor. Add the basil leaves and process until very finely chopped. You may need to scrape down the sides of the bowl with a spatula.

2 Cut the tomatoes in half and add them to the shallot mixture. Pulse until the mixture is well blended and the tomatoes are finely chopped.

3 With the motor still running, slowly pour in the olive oil through the feeder tube. Add salt and pepper to taste and pulse briefly to mix. Spoon the mixture into a bowl.

4 Cut the chillies lengthways and scrape out the seeds with a sharp knife and discard. Finely slice across the chillies, cutting them into tiny strips and stir them into the tomato mixture. Garnish with a few torn basil leaves. Serve the dip at room temperature. Refrigerated, this will keep for 3–4 days.

CHILLI BEAN DIP

SUBSTANTIAL ENOUGH TO SERVE FOR SUPPER ON A BAKED POTATO, THIS CREAMY BEAN DIP ALSO TASTES GREAT WITH TRIANGLES OF LIGHTLY TOASTED PITTA BREAD OR A BOWL OF CRUNCHY TORTILLA CHIPS. SERVE IT WARM TO ENJOY IT AT ITS BEST.

SERVES FOUR

INGREDIENTS

2 fresh green chillies
2 garlic cloves
1 onion
30ml/2 tbsp vegetable oil
5–10ml/1–2 tsp hot chilli powder
400g/14oz can kidney beans
75g/3oz/¾ cup grated (shredded)
  mature (sharp) Cheddar cheese
1 fresh red chilli, seeded
salt and ground black pepper

1 Slit the green chillies and use a sharp knife to scrape out the seeds. Chop the flesh finely, then crush the garlic and finely chop the onion.

2 Heat the oil in a large pan and add the garlic, onion, green chillies and chilli powder. Cook gently for 5 minutes, stirring, until the onions have softened and are transparent, but not browned.

COOK'S TIP
Fresh green chillies provide the heat in this dip. You can substitute sweet red (bell) pepper for the garnish.

3 Drain the kidney beans, reserving the liquid in which they were canned. Set aside 30ml/2 tbsp of the beans and purée the remainder in a food processor or blender.

4 Spoon the puréed beans into the pan and stir in 30–45ml/2–3 tbsp of the reserved can liquid. Heat gently, stirring to mix well.

5 Stir in the reserved whole kidney beans and the Cheddar cheese. Cook gently for 2–3 minutes, stirring regularly until the cheese melts. Add salt and pepper to taste.

6 Cut the red chilli into tiny strips. Spoon the dip into 4 individual serving bowls and sprinkle the chilli strips over the top. Serve warm.

COCONUT CHUTNEY WITH ONION AND CHILLI

SERVE THIS REFRESHING COCONUT CHUTNEY AS AN ACCOMPANIMENT TO INDIAN-STYLE DISHES OR AT THE START OF A MEAL, WITH POPPADUMS, A RAITA AND OTHER CHUTNEYS.

SERVES FOUR TO SIX

INGREDIENTS
  200g/7oz fresh coconut, grated
  3–4 fresh green chillies, seeded
    and chopped
  60ml/4 tbsp chopped fresh
    coriander (cilantro)
  30ml/2 tbsp chopped fresh mint
  30–45ml/2–3 tbsp lime juice
  about 2.5ml/½ tsp salt
  about 2.5ml/½ tsp granulated sugar
  15–30ml/1–2 tbsp coconut milk
  30ml/2 tbsp groundnut
    (peanut) oil
  5ml/1 tsp kalonji (nigella seeds)
  1 small onion, very finely chopped
  fresh coriander (cilantro) sprigs,
    to garnish

1 Place the coconut, chillies, coriander and mint in a food processor. Add 30ml/2 tbsp of the lime juice, then process until thoroughly chopped.

2 Scrape the mixture into a bowl. Stir in more lime juice to taste, with the salt, sugar and coconut milk.

3 Heat the oil in a small pan and fry the kalonji until they begin to pop. Reduce the heat and add the onion. Fry, stirring frequently, until the onion is soft.

4 Stir the spiced onions into the coconut mixture and cool. Garnish with coriander sprigs before serving.

ONION, MANGO AND CHILLI CHAAT

CHAATS ARE SPICED RELISHES OF VEGETABLES AND NUTS SERVED WITH INDIAN MEALS. USE GREEN JALAPEÑOS OR SERRANOS FOR MEDIUM HEAT, OR GREEN CAYENNE CHILLIES IF YOU WANT IT HOT.

SERVES FOUR

INGREDIENTS
  15ml/1 tbsp groundnut (peanut) oil
  90g/3½oz/1 cup unsalted peanuts
  1 onion, chopped
  10cm/4in piece cucumber, seeded
    and cut into 5mm/¼in dice
  1 mango, peeled, stoned (pitted)
    and diced
  1–2 fresh green chillies, seeded and
    finely chopped
  30ml/2 tbsp chopped fresh
    coriander (cilantro)
  15ml/1 tbsp chopped fresh mint
  15ml/1 tbsp lime juice
  pinch of granulated sugar
For the chaat masala
  10ml/2 tsp ground toasted
    cumin seeds
  2.5ml/½ tsp cayenne pepper
  5ml/1 tsp mango powder (amchoor)
  2.5ml/½ tsp garam masala
  salt and ground black pepper

1 To make the chaat masala, grind all the spices together, then season with 2.5ml/½ tsp each of salt and pepper.

2 Heat the oil in a small pan and fry the peanuts until lightly browned, then drain on kitchen paper and set aside until cool.

COOK'S TIP
Mango powder (amchoor) is made by grinding sun-dried mango slices and mixing the powder with a little turmeric.

3 Mix the onion, cucumber, mango, chilli, fresh coriander and mint. Sprinkle in 5ml/1 tsp of the chaat masala. Stir in the peanuts and then add the lime juice and sugar to taste. Set the mixture aside for 20–30 minutes for the flavours to mature.

4 Spoon the mixture into a serving bowl, sprinkle another 5ml/1 tsp of the chaat masala over and serve. Any remaining chaat masala will keep in a sealed jar for 4–6 weeks.

CHILLI RELISH

FOR INSTANT HEAT, KEEP A POT OF THIS SPICY RELISH. IT TASTES GREAT WITH SAUSAGES, BURGERS AND CHEESE. IT WILL KEEP IN THE REFRIGERATOR FOR UP TO TWO WEEKS.

SERVES EIGHT

INGREDIENTS
  6 tomatoes
  1 onion
  1 sweet red (bell) pepper, seeded
  2 garlic cloves
  30ml/2 tbsp olive oil
  5ml/1 tsp ground cinnamon
  5ml/1 tsp dried chilli flakes
  5ml/1 tsp ground ginger
  5ml/1 tsp salt
  2.5ml/½ tsp ground black pepper
  75g/3oz/scant ⅔ cup light muscovado
    (brown) sugar
  75ml/5 tbsp cider vinegar
  handful of fresh basil leaves

COOK'S TIP
This relish thickens slightly on cooling, so do not worry if the mixture seems a little sloppy when it is first made.

1 Skewer each of the tomatoes in turn on a metal fork and hold in a gas flame for 1–2 minutes, turning until the skin splits and wrinkles. Place the tomatoes on a chopping board, slip off the skins, then roughly chop.

2 Roughly chop the onion, red pepper and garlic. Gently heat the oil in a pan. Tip in the onion, red pepper and garlic, stirring lightly.

3 Cook gently for 5–8 minutes, until the pepper has softened. Add the chopped tomatoes, cover and cook for 5 minutes.

4 Stir in the cinnamon, chilli flakes, ginger, salt, pepper, sugar and vinegar. Bring gently to the boil, stirring until the sugar dissolves.

5 Simmer, uncovered, for 20 minutes, until the mixture is pulpy. Stir in the basil leaves and check the seasoning.

6 Allow to cool completely, then spoon into a glass jar or a plastic tub with a tightly fitting lid. Store, covered, in the refrigerator. This relish will keep in the refrigerator for up to a fortnight. Stir before using.

SPICY SWEETCORN RELISH

A TOUCH OF HEAT TEMPERS THE SWEETNESS OF THIS DELICIOUS RELISH. TRY IT WITH CRISP ONION BHAJIS OR SLICES OF HONEY-ROAST HAM FOR A SPICY SNACK.

SERVES FOUR

INGREDIENTS
1 large onion
1 fresh red chilli, seeded
2 garlic cloves
30ml/2 tbsp vegetable oil
5ml/1 tsp black mustard seeds
10ml/2 tsp hot curry powder
320g/11¼oz can sweetcorn
grated rind and juice of 1 lime
45ml/3 tbsp chopped fresh
  coriander (cilantro)
salt and ground black pepper

1 Chop the onion, chilli and garlic. Heat the vegetable oil in a large frying pan and cook the onion, chilli and garlic over a high heat for 5 minutes, until the onions are just beginning to brown.

2 Stir in the mustard seeds and curry powder. Cook for a further 2 minutes, stirring, until all the seeds start to splutter and the onions have browned.

COOK'S TIP
Opt for canned rather than frozen sweetcorn if possible, as the kernels are plump, moist and ready to eat.

3 Remove the fried onion mixture from the heat and allow to cool. Place in a glass bowl. Drain the sweetcorn and stir it into the onion mixture.

4 Add the lime rind and juice, coriander and salt and pepper to taste. Cover and refrigerate until needed. The relish is best served at room temperature.

Starting with a hint of heat sets the scene for

an exciting meal. Pulses race at the taste of a

spiced red lentil soup, but the effect is softened

by coconut, which also tames the chillies in a

hearty African offering. Classic favourites

like wontons and ceviche sparkle when given

the chilli treatment, while flash-fried squid

positively sizzles.

Soups and Appetizers

WARMING SPINACH AND RICE SOUP

THE CHILLI ADDS JUST A FLICKER OF FIRE TO THIS LIGHT AND FRESH-TASTING SOUP, MADE USING VERY YOUNG SPINACH LEAVES AND RISOTTO RICE.

SERVES FOUR

INGREDIENTS
675g/1½lb fresh spinach, washed
45ml/3 tbsp extra virgin olive oil
1 small onion, finely chopped
2 garlic cloves, finely chopped
1 small fresh red chilli, seeded and
  finely chopped
115g/4oz/generous ½ cup risotto rice
1.2 litres/2 pints/5 cups
  vegetable stock
60ml/4 tbsp grated (shredded)
  Pecorino cheese
salt and ground black pepper

1 Place the spinach in a large pan with just the water that clings to its leaves. Add a pinch of salt. Heat until the spinach has wilted, then remove from the heat and drain, reserving any liquid.

2 Either chop the spinach finely using a large knife or place in a food processor and process briefly to achieve a fairly coarse purée.

3 Heat the oil in a large pan and gently cook the onion, garlic and chilli for 4–5 minutes until softened but not browned. Stir in the risotto rice until well coated with the mixture.

4 Pour in the stock and reserved spinach liquid. Bring to the boil, reduce the heat and simmer for 10 minutes.

5 Add the spinach, with salt and pepper to taste. Cook for 5–7 minutes more, until the rice is tender. Check the seasoning and serve in heated soup plates or bowls, with the Pecorino cheese sprinkled over.

SPICED RED LENTIL AND COCONUT SOUP

HOT, SPICY AND RICHLY FLAVOURED, THIS SUBSTANTIAL SOUP IS ALMOST A MEAL IN ITSELF. IF YOU ARE REALLY HUNGRY, SERVE IT WITH CHUNKS OF WARMED NAAN BREAD OR THICK SLICES OF TOAST.

SERVES FOUR

INGREDIENTS
  30ml/2 tbsp sunflower oil
  2 red onions, finely chopped
  1 bird's eye chilli, seeded and
    finely sliced
  2 garlic cloves, chopped
  1 lemon grass stalk, outer layers
    removed and inside finely sliced
  200g/7oz/scant 1 cup red lentils,
    rinsed and drained
  5ml/1 tsp ground coriander
  5ml/1 tsp paprika
  400ml/14fl oz/1⅔ cups
    coconut milk
  900ml/1½ pints/3¾ cups water
  juice of 1 lime
  3 spring onions (scallions), chopped
  20g/¾oz/½ cup fresh coriander
    (cilantro), finely chopped
  salt and ground black pepper

1 Heat the oil in a large pan and add the onions, chilli, garlic and lemon grass. Cook for 5 minutes or until the onions have softened but not browned, stirring occasionally.

COOK'S TIP
Bird's eye chillies may look insubstantial, but they pack quite a punch. Don't be tempted to add more unless you are a real *chillihead!*

2 Add the lentils and spices. Pour in the coconut milk and water, and stir. Bring to the boil, stir, then reduce the heat and simmer for 40–45 minutes or until the lentils are soft and mushy.

3 Stir in the lime juice and add the spring onions and fresh coriander, reserving a little of each for the garnish. Season, then ladle into heated bowls. Top with the reserved garnishes.

PUMPKIN SOUP WITH ANIS

USE MILD CHILLIES FOR THIS TASTY SOUP, SO THAT THEY ACCENTUATE THE PUMPKIN FLAVOUR AND DO NOT MASK THE LIQUORICE TASTE OF THE ANISEED-FLAVOURED APERITIF.

SERVES FOUR

INGREDIENTS

1 pumpkin, about 675g/1½lb
30ml/2 tbsp olive oil
2 large onions, sliced
1 garlic clove, crushed
2 fresh red chillies, seeded
  and chopped
5ml/1 tsp curry paste
1 litre/1¾ pints/4 cups vegetable or
  chicken stock
15ml/1 tbsp Anis, Pernod, or aniseed
  (anise seed)-flavoured aperitif
150ml/¼ pint/⅔ cup single
  (light) cream
salt and ground black pepper

1 Peel the pumpkin with a sturdy knife, cutting the skin away from the flesh, remove the seeds and then chop the flesh roughly.

2 Heat the oil in a pan and fry the onions until golden. Stir in the garlic, chillies and curry paste. Cook for 1 minute, then add the chopped pumpkin and cook for 5 minutes more, stirring frequently to prevent browning.

3 Pour over the stock and season with salt and pepper. Bring to the boil, reduce the heat, cover and simmer for about 25 minutes.

4 Spoon about one-third of the soup into a blender or food processor, process until smooth, then scrape into a clean pan. Repeat with the remaining soup, processing it in 2 batches.

5 Add the anis and reheat. Taste and season if necessary with salt and pepper. Serve the soup in individual heated bowls, adding a spoonful of cream to each portion.

VEGETABLE SOUP <u>WITH</u> CHILLI <u>AND</u> COCONUT

ALL OVER AFRICA, CHILLIES PLAY AN IMPORTANT PART IN THE CUISINE. IN THIS HEARTY VEGETABLE SOUP, CHILLI IS PARTNERED WITH OTHER WARMING SPICES.

SERVES FOUR

INGREDIENTS
 ½ red onion
 175g/6oz each of turnip, sweet
   potato and pumpkin
 30ml/2 tbsp butter
 5ml/1 tsp dried marjoram
 2.5ml/½ tsp ground ginger
 1.5ml/¼ tsp ground cinnamon
 15ml/1 tbsp chopped spring
   onion (scallion)
 1 litre/1¾ pint/4 cups well-flavoured
   vegetable stock
 30ml/2 tbsp flaked (sliced) almonds
 1 fresh red chilli, seeded
   and chopped
 5ml/1 tsp granulated sugar
 25g/1oz creamed coconut
   (coconut cream)
 salt and ground black pepper
 chopped fresh coriander (cilantro),
   to garnish (optional)

1 Finely chop the onion, then peel the turnip, sweet potato and pumpkin and cut into 1cm/½in dice.

2 Melt the butter in a large non-stick pan. Fry the onion for 4–5 minutes. Add the diced vegetables and fry for 3–4 minutes.

3 Stir in the marjoram, ginger, cinnamon and spring onion with salt and pepper to taste. Fry over a low heat for about 10 minutes, stirring frequently.

COOK'S TIP
Choose young small turnips. The flavour will have a nutty sweetness.

4 Pour in the vegetable stock and add the almonds, chopped chilli and sugar. Stir well to mix, then cover and simmer gently for 10–15 minutes until the vegetables are just tender.

5 Grate the creamed coconut into the soup and stir gently to mix. Sprinkle with the chopped coriander, if you like, and spoon into heated bowls and serve.

TORTILLA SOUP

THE SOUTH-WESTERN UNITED STATES STAKES ITS CLAIM TO THIS SIMPLE AND DELICIOUS SOUP, BUT IT PROBABLY ORIGINATED IN MEXICO, WHERE CONSIDERABLY HOTTER VERSIONS ARE POPULAR.

SERVES FOUR TO SIX

INGREDIENTS
15ml/1 tbsp vegetable oil
1 onion, finely chopped
1 large garlic clove, crushed
2 medium tomatoes, peeled, seeded
   and chopped
2.5ml/½ tsp salt
2 litres/3½ pints/8 cups
   chicken stock
1 carrot, diced
1 courgette (zucchini), diced
1 skinless, boneless chicken breast
   portion, cooked and shredded
1 fresh green chilli, seeded
   and chopped
To garnish
4 corn tortillas
oil, for frying
1 small ripe avocado, peeled, stoned
   (pitted) and diced
2 spring onions (scallions),
   finely chopped
chopped fresh coriander (cilantro)
grated Cheddar or Monterey Jack
   cheese (optional)

1 Heat the oil in a large pan and fry the onion and garlic over a medium heat for 5–8 minutes until softened. Stir in the tomatoes and salt, and cook for 5 minutes more.

2 Stir in the stock. Bring to the boil, then cover, reduce the heat and simmer for about 15 minutes.

COOK'S TIP
To make stock, put a chicken carcass in a large pan, add water to cover, 2 chopped onions, a stick of celery and some peppercorns. Bring to the boil, cover, simmer for 40 minutes then strain.

3 Meanwhile, for the garnish, trim the tortillas into squares, then cut into strips.

4 Pour oil into a frying pan to a depth of about 1cm/½in. Heat until hot but not smoking. Add the tortilla strips, in batches, and fry until just beginning to brown. Remove with a slotted spoon and drain on kitchen paper.

5 Add the carrot to the soup. Cook, covered, for 10 minutes. Add the courgette, chicken and chilli, and continue cooking for about 5 minutes, until the vegetables are just tender.

6 Divide the tortilla strips among 4–6 heated soup bowls. Sprinkle with the avocado. Ladle in the soup, then arrange spring onions and coriander on top. Serve with grated cheese if you like.

VARIATION
Parmesan balls make a nice alternative to shredded cheese. Grate 25g/1oz Parmesan and mix well with 2 egg yolks. When the soup is ready to serve, drop half teaspoons of the mixture all over the surface. Leave for 2–3 minutes or until just firm, then serve.

SPICED MUSSEL SOUP

CHUNKY AND COLOURFUL, THIS FISH SOUP HAS THE CONSISTENCY OF A CHOWDER. THE CHILLI FLAVOUR COMES FROM HARISSA, A SPICY SAUCE THAT IS POPULAR IN NORTH AFRICAN COOKING.

SERVES SIX

INGREDIENTS

1.6kg/3½lb live mussels
150ml/¼ pint/⅔ cup white wine
3 tomatoes
30ml/2 tbsp olive oil
1 onion, finely chopped
2 garlic cloves, crushed
2 celery sticks, thinly sliced
bunch of spring onions (scallions),
  thinly sliced
1 potato, diced
7.5ml/1½ tsp harissa
45ml/3 tbsp chopped fresh parsley
ground black pepper
thick yogurt, to serve (optional)

1 Scrub the mussels and remove the beards, discarding any mussels that are damaged or that fail to close when tapped with a knife.

2 Bring the wine to the boil in a large pan. Add the mussels and cover tightly with a lid. Cook for 4–5 minutes until the mussels have opened. Drain the mussels, reserving the cooking liquid. Discard any mussels that remain closed. Reserve a few mussels in their shells for the garnish. Shell the rest.

3 Cut a small cross in the base of each tomato. Put them in a heatproof bowl and pour over boiling water. Leave for 30 seconds, then lift out and plunge into cold water. Drain, peel off the skins and dice the flesh. Heat the oil in a pan and fry the onion, garlic, celery and spring onions for 5 minutes.

COOK'S TIP
Harissa can be bought in tubes or jars. Stir it into salads or cooked vegetable dishes to give them a spicy lift.

4 Add the shelled mussels, reserved liquid, potato, harissa and tomatoes. Bring just to the boil, reduce the heat and cover. Simmer gently for about 25 minutes, or until the potatoes are beginning to break up.

5 Stir in the parsley and pepper, and add the reserved mussels, in their shells. Heat through for 1 minute. Serve with a spoonful of yogurt if you like.

THAI-STYLE MARINATED SALMON

MADE IN A SIMILAR FASHION TO THE SCANDINAVIAN SPECIALITY, GRAVLAX, THIS IS A WONDERFUL WAY OF PREPARING SALMON. START THE PREPARATION TWO TO FIVE DAYS BEFORE YOU INTEND TO EAT IT.

SERVES FOUR TO SIX

INGREDIENTS
    tail piece of 1 salmon, about
        675g/1½lb, cleaned and prepared
        (see below)
    20ml/4 tsp coarse sea salt
    20ml/4 tsp granulated sugar
    2.5cm/1in piece fresh root
        ginger, grated (shredded)
    2 lemon grass stalks
    4 kaffir lime leaves, finely chopped
        or shredded
    grated (shredded) rind of
        1 kaffir lime
    1 fresh red chilli, seeded and
        finely chopped
    5ml/1 tsp black peppercorns,
        coarsely crushed
    30ml/2 tbsp chopped fresh coriander
        (cilantro), plus sprigs to garnish
    wedges of kaffir lime, to garnish
For the dressing
    150ml/¼ pint/⅔ cup mayonnaise
    juice of ½ lime
    10ml/2 tsp chopped fresh
        coriander (cilantro)

1 Ask your fishmonger to scale the fish and remove the skin, splitting the fish lengthways to remove it from the backbone in 2 matching fillets. Use tweezers to remove all the bones from the salmon.

2 In a bowl, mix together the salt, sugar and ginger. Remove the outer leaves from the lemon grass and slice the inner portion finely. Add to the bowl, with the lime leaves, lime rind, chilli, peppercorns and coriander.

3 Place one-quarter of the spice mixture in a shallow dish. Place one salmon fillet, skin-side down, on top of the spices. Spread two-thirds of the remaining mixture over the flesh then place the remaining fillet on top, flesh-side down. Arrange the rest of the spice mixture over the fish.

COOK'S TIP
Kaffir lime leaves and the rind of the fruit are very aromatic and a distinctive feature of Thai cooking. They should be available from Asian food stores. If not, substitute ordinary limes.

4 Cover the fish with foil, then place a board on top. Add some weights, such as clean cans of food. Chill for 2–5 days, turning the fish each day in the spicy marinade to ensure that the flavour permeates all parts of the fish.

5 Make the dressing by mixing the mayonnaise, lime juice and chopped coriander in a bowl.

6 Scrape the spices off the fish. Slice it as thinly as possible. Serve with the lime dressing, garnished with fresh coriander and wedges of kaffir lime.

CEVICHE

FRESH FISH IS "COOKED" BY BEING MARINATED IN A MIXTURE OF MANGO, LIME JUICE AND CHILLIES. THE RESULT IS AN APPETIZER WITH A WONDERFULLY FRESH FLAVOUR.

SERVES SIX

INGREDIENTS
  350g/12oz medium cooked
    prawns (shrimp)
  350g/12oz scallops, removed from
    their shells, with corals intact
  2 tomatoes, about 175g/6oz
  1 red onion, finely chopped
  1 small mango
  350g/12oz salmon fillet
  1 fresh red chilli
  12 limes
  30ml/2 tbsp caster (superfine) sugar
  2 pink grapefruit
  3 oranges
  salt and ground black pepper
  lime slices, to garnish (optional)

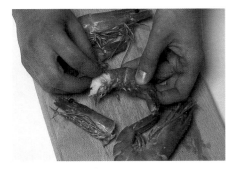

1 Peel the prawns and place them in a large bowl. Cut the scallop meat into 1cm/½in dice. Add it to the bowl.

2 Dice the tomatoes. Peel the mango and cut off a thick slice close to the flat side of the stone (pit). Repeat on the other side. Score the flesh with criss-cross lines, then fold the slices inside out so the dice stand proud of the skin. Slice these off the skin and into a bowl.

3 Skin the salmon, if necessary, then cut it into small pieces. Slit the chilli and scrape out and discard the seeds. Dice the flesh. Add the tomatoes, mango, salmon, chilli and onion to the shellfish in the bowl.

4 Squeeze 8 of the limes and add the juice to the bowl, with the sugar and seasoning. Stir, cover and leave the ceviche to marinate for 3 hours in the refrigerator.

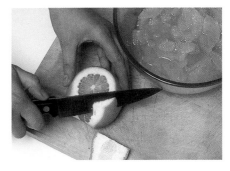

5 Segment the grapefruit, oranges and remaining limes. Drain off as much excess lime juice as possible from the marinated fish and gently fold in the fruit segments. Season to taste and arrange on a platter. Garnish with lime slices, if you like. Serve immediately.

COOK'S TIP
Take very special care in choosing the fish for this dish; it must be very fresh and served on the day it is prepared.

PAN-STEAMED CHILLI MUSSELS

IF YOU CAN TAKE THE HEAT, USE BIRD'S EYE CHILLIES FOR THIS SIMPLE DISH, OR SUBSTITUTE ONE RED CAYENNE OR TWO RED FRESNO CHILLIES. THE LEMON GRASS ADDS A REFRESHING TANG.

2 Cut off the lower 5cm/2in of each lemon grass stalk and chop finely. Add to the pan, with the shallots, kaffir lime leaves, chillies, Thai fish sauce and lime juice.

3 Cover the pan with a lid and place it over medium-high heat. Steam for 5–7 minutes, shaking the pan occasionally, until the mussels open. Discard any of the mussels that have not opened.

SERVES FOUR TO SIX

INGREDIENTS
  1kg/2¼lb live mussels
  2 lemon grass stalks
  4 shallots, chopped
  4 kaffir lime leaves, roughly torn
  1–2 fresh red chillies, seeded
    and sliced
  15ml/1 tbsp Thai fish sauce
    (*nam pla*)
  30ml/2 tbsp lime juice
  2 spring onions (scallions), chopped,
    to garnish
  coriander (cilantro) leaves,
    to garnish

1 Scrub the mussels and remove the beards, discarding any mussels that are damaged or that fail to close when tapped with a knife. Place in a large heavy pan.

4 Using a slotted spoon, transfer the cooked mussels to a serving dish, along with any liquid that has been produced. Garnish with chopped spring onions and coriander leaves. Serve immediately.

FLASH-FRIED SQUID WITH PAPRIKA AND GARLIC

THESE QUICK-FRIED SQUID ARE GOOD SERVED WITH A DRY SHERRY OR MANZANILLA AS AN APPETIZER OR AS PART OF MIXED TAPAS. FOR A FIRST COURSE, SERVE THEM ON A BED OF SALAD LEAVES.

SERVES FOUR TO SIX

INGREDIENTS
    500g/1¼lb very small squid, cleaned
    90ml/6 tbsp olive oil
    1 fresh red chilli, seeded and
      finely chopped
    10ml/2 tsp Spanish mild smoked
      paprika (*pimentón dulce*)
    30ml/2 tbsp plain (all-purpose) flour
    2 garlic cloves, finely chopped
    15ml/1 tbsp sherry vinegar
    5ml/1 tsp shredded lemon rind
    30–45ml/2–3 tbsp finely chopped
      fresh parsley
    salt and ground black pepper
    salad leaves, to serve (optional)

1 Choose small squid that are no longer than 10cm/4in. Cut the body sacs into rings and cut the tentacles into bitesize pieces.

2 Place the squid in a bowl and add 30ml/2 tbsp of the oil, half the chilli and the paprika. Season with a little salt and some pepper, cover and marinate for 2–4 hours in the refrigerator.

COOK'S TIPS
• Make sure the wok or pan is very hot, as the squid should cook for only 1–2 minutes: any longer and it will begin to toughen.
• Smoked paprika, known as *pimentón dulce* in Spain, has a wonderful smoky flavour. If you cannot find it, use mild paprika, which should be described as such on the packet.

3 Heat the remaining oil in a preheated wok or fairly deep frying pan over a high heat until very hot. Toss the squid in the flour and divide it into 2 batches. Add the first batch of squid to the wok or frying pan and stir-fry quickly, turning the squid constantly for 1–2 minutes, or until the squid rings become opaque and the tentacles have curled.

4 Sprinkle in half the garlic. Stir to mix then turn out on to a plate and keep warm. Repeat the stir-frying with the second batch of squid and garlic.

5 Sprinkle the sherry vinegar, lemon rind, remaining chilli and parsley over the squid. Taste for seasoning and serve hot or cool, on a bed of salad leaves, if you like.

PERI-PERI PRAWNS WITH AIOLI

THE NAME PERI-PERI REFERS TO THE SMALL, EXTREMELY HOT ANGOLAN CHILLIES FROM WHICH THIS PORTUGUESE DISH IS TRADITIONALLY MADE. ANY SMALL HOT CHILLI CAN BE USED INSTEAD.

SERVES FOUR

INGREDIENTS
    1 fresh red chilli (such as bird's eye),
        seeded and finely chopped
    2.5ml/½ tsp paprika
    2.5ml/½ tsp ground coriander
    1 garlic clove, crushed
    juice of ½ lime
    30ml/2 tbsp olive oil
    20 large raw prawns (shrimp) in
        shells, heads removed and deveined
    salt and ground black pepper
    whole chillies, to garnish (optional)
For the aioli (quick method)
    150ml/¼ pint/⅔ cup mayonnaise
    2 garlic cloves, crushed
    5ml/1 tsp Dijon mustard
For the aioli (classic method)
    2 egg yolks
    2 crushed garlic cloves
    5ml/1 tsp granulated sugar
    5ml/1 tsp Dijon mustard
    10ml/2 tsp lemon juice
    250ml/8fl oz/1 cup mixed olive oil
        and sunflower oil

1 To make the aioli by the quick method, mix the mayonnaise, garlic and mustard in a small bowl and set aside. For the classic method, put the egg yolks in a blender or food processor and add the garlic, sugar, mustard and lemon juice. Process until mixed, then, with the motor running, add the oil through the hole in the lid or feeder tube, drip by drip at first, then in a steady stream, until all the oil has been added and the aioli is smooth.
Any dish that contains raw egg should not be served to young children, pregnant women or the elderly.

2 Make a peri-peri marinade by mixing the chilli, paprika, coriander, garlic, lime juice and olive oil in a non-metallic bowl. Add salt and pepper to taste. Pour over the prawns and mix well. Cover and leave in a cool place to marinate for 30 minutes, turning the prawns in the mixture from time to time.

3 Thread the prawns on to metal skewers and cook under the grill (broiler) or on the barbecue, basting and turning frequently, for 6–8 minutes until pink. Serve with the aioli, garnished with extra chillies, if you like.

SPICY SHELLFISH WONTONS

THESE TASTY WONTONS LOOK A BIT LIKE TORTELLINI BUT THE TASTE IS MORE THAI THAN TRIESTE. WATER CHESTNUTS ADD A LIGHT CRUNCH TO THE CRAB AND CHILLI FILLING.

SERVES FOUR

INGREDIENTS

225g/8oz raw prawns (shrimp),
   peeled and deveined
115g/4oz white crab meat,
   picked over
4 drained canned water chestnuts,
   finely diced
1 spring onion (scallion),
   finely chopped
1 small fresh green chilli, seeded and
   finely chopped
1.5ml/¼ tsp grated (shredded) fresh
   root ginger
1 egg, separated
20–24 wonton wrappers
salt and ground black pepper
coriander (cilantro) leaves, to garnish
For the dressing
   30ml/2 tbsp rice vinegar
   15ml/1 tbsp chopped pickled ginger
   90ml/6 tbsp olive oil
   15ml1/ tbsp soy sauce
   45ml/3 tbsp chopped
      coriander (cilantro)
   30ml/2 tbsp diced red (bell) pepper

1 Finely dice the prawns and place them in a bowl. Stir in the next 5 ingredients and the egg white. Season with salt and pepper and mix well.

2 Place a wonton wrapper on a board. Put about 5ml/1 tsp of the filling just above the centre of the wrapper. With a pastry brush, moisten the edges of the wrapper with a little of the egg yolk. Bring the bottom of the wrapper up over the filling. Press gently to expel any air, then seal neatly in a triangle.

3 For a more elaborate shape, bring the 2 side points up over the filling, overlap the points and pinch the ends firmly together. Space the filled wontons on a large baking sheet lined with greaseproof (waxed) paper, so that they do not stick together.

4 Half-fill a large pan with water. Bring to simmering point. Add the filled wontons, a few at a time, and simmer for 2–3 minutes. The wontons will float to the surface and when they are cooked and ready to remove, the wrappers will be translucent and the filling cooked. Remove the wontons with a large slotted spoon, drain them briefly, then spread them on trays. Keep warm while cooking the remaining wontons.

5 Make the dressing by whisking all the ingredients together in a bowl. Divide the warm wontons among 4 serving dishes, drizzle with the spicy dressing and serve garnished with a handful of coriander leaves.

If you are serving just a single course you can safely

turn up the heat without the risk of dulling the palate

to the delights of a delicate dessert. Chillies Rellenos,

Quesadillas and Chicken Flautas with Fresno Chilli

Salsa are Mexican specialities packed with flavour

and fire, while Chicken Satay and Three-colour Fish

Kebabs are milder but just as tasty.

Snacks and Light Meals

CHILLIES RELLENOS

STUFFED CHILLIES ARE POPULAR ALL OVER MEXICO. THE TYPE OF CHILLI USED DIFFERS FROM REGION TO REGION, BUT LARGER CHILLIES ARE OBVIOUSLY EASIER TO STUFF THAN SMALLER ONES.

MAKES SIX

INGREDIENTS

6 fresh poblano or Anaheim chillies
2 potatoes, total weight about
  400g/14oz
200g/7oz/scant 1 cup cream cheese
200g/7oz/1¾ cups grated (shredded)
  mature (sharp) Cheddar cheese
5ml/1 tsp salt
2.5ml/½ tsp ground black pepper
2 eggs, separated
115g/4oz/1 cup plain
  (all-purpose) flour
2.5ml/½ tsp white pepper
oil, for frying
dried chilli flakes, to garnish (optional)

1 Make a neat slit down one side of each chilli. Place them in a dry frying pan over a medium heat, turning them frequently until the skins blister.

2 Place the chillies in a strong plastic bag and tie the top to keep the steam in. Set aside for 20 minutes, then carefully peel off the skins and remove the seeds through the slits, keeping the chillies whole. Dry the chillies with kitchen paper and set them aside.

COOK'S TIP
Take care when making the filling; mix gently, in order to avoid breaking up the diced potato.

VARIATION
Whole ancho (dried poblano) chillies can be used instead of fresh chillies, but will need to be reconstituted in water before they can be seeded and stuffed.

3 Scrub or peel the potatoes and cut them into 1cm/½in dice. Bring a large pan of water to the boil, add the potatoes and let the water return to boiling point. Lower the heat and simmer for 5 minutes or until the potatoes are just tender. Do not overcook. Drain them thoroughly.

4 Put the cream cheese in a bowl and stir in the grated Cheddar cheese, with 2.5ml/½ tsp of the salt and all the black pepper. Add the par-cooked potato and mix gently.

5 Spoon some of the potato filling into each chilli. Put them on a plate, cover with clear film (plastic wrap) and chill for 1 hour so the filling becomes firm.

6 Put the egg whites in a clean, grease-free bowl and whisk them to firm, dry peaks. In a separate bowl, beat the yolks until pale, then carefully fold in the whites. Scrape the mixture into a large, shallow dish. Spread out the plain flour in another large shallow dish and season it with the remaining salt and the white pepper.

7 Heat the oil for frying to 190°C/375°F. Coat a few chillies first in seasoned flour and then in egg before adding carefully to the hot oil.

8 Fry the chillies in batches until golden and crisp. Drain on kitchen paper and serve hot, garnished with a sprinkle of chilli flakes, if you like.

PARTY PIZZETTES <u>WITH A HINT OF</u> CHILLI

BRUSHING PIZZA DOUGH WITH CHILLI OIL BEFORE ADDING A FLAVOURSOME TOPPING GIVES A TANTALIZING SUGGESTION OF WARMTH WHEN YOU BITE INTO THESE DELICIOUS SNACKS.

SERVES FOUR

INGREDIENTS
   150g/5oz packet pizza dough mix
   5ml/1 tsp salt
   120ml/4fl oz/½ cup lukewarm water
   30ml/2 tbsp chilli oil
   75g/3oz mozzarella cheese, grated
   1 garlic clove, chopped
   ½ small red onion, thinly sliced
   4–6 pieces sun-dried tomatoes in oil,
     drained and thinly sliced
   115g/4oz cooked, peeled
     prawns (shrimp)
   30ml/2 tbsp chopped fresh basil
   salt and ground black pepper
   shredded basil leaves, to garnish

1 Preheat the oven to 220ºC/425ºF/ Gas 7. Tip the pizza dough mix into a mixing bowl and stir in the salt. Pour in the water and mix to a soft dough.

2 Knead the dough on a lightly floured surface for 5 minutes until smooth and elastic. Divide it into 8 equal pieces.

3 Roll out each piece to a small oval 5mm/¼in thick. Place well apart on 2 greased baking sheets.

4 Prick each of the pizza bases all over with a fork and brush lightly with 15ml/1 tbsp of the chilli oil. Top with the grated mozzarella cheese, being careful to leave a 1cm/½in border all round.

5 Divide the garlic, onion, sun-dried tomatoes, prawns and basil among the pizza bases. Season and drizzle over the remaining chilli oil. Bake for 8–10 minutes until crisp and golden. Garnish with basil leaves and serve immediately.

CHILLI, TOMATO AND SPINACH PIZZA

THIS RICHLY FLAVOURED TOPPING WITH A HINT OF SPICE MAKES A COLOURFUL AND SATISFYING PIZZA. ADDED TO A READY-MADE PIZZA BASE, IT MAKES THE COOK'S LIFE REALLY EASY.

SERVES THREE

INGREDIENTS
1–2 fresh red chillies
50g/2oz/½ cup sun-dried tomatoes in oil, drained, plus 45ml/3 tbsp oil from the jar
1 onion, chopped
2 garlic cloves, chopped
400g/14oz can chopped tomatoes
15ml/1 tbsp tomato purée (paste)
175g/6oz fresh spinach
1 ready-made pizza base, 25–30cm/10–12in in diameter
75g/3oz/¾ cup grated (shredded) smoked Bavarian cheese
75g/3oz/¾ cup grated (shredded) mature (sharp) Cheddar cheese
salt and ground black pepper

1 Slit the chillies, open them out and use a sharp knife to scrape out the seeds. Chop the flesh finely.

2 Heat 30ml/2 tbsp of the oil from the sun-dried tomatoes in a pan, add the chopped onion, garlic and chillies, and fry gently for about 5 minutes until the onions are soft. Do not let them brown.

3 Roughly chop the sun-dried tomatoes. Add them to the pan with the canned chopped tomatoes, tomato purée and seasoning. Simmer uncovered, stirring occasionally, for 15 minutes.

4 Preheat the oven to 220°C/425°F/ Gas 7. Remove the stalks from the spinach and wash the leaves in plenty of cold water. Drain well and pat dry with kitchen paper. Roughly chop the spinach.

5 Add the spinach to the sauce and stir gently. Cook, stirring, for a further 5–10 minutes until the spinach has wilted and no excess moisture remains.

6 Brush the pizza base with the remaining tomato oil, then spoon over the sauce. Sprinkle over the cheeses and bake for 15–20 minutes or for the time recommended on the packaging of the pizza base, until crisp and golden. Serve immediately.

QUESADILLAS

FILLED WITH CHEESE AND CHILLIES, THESE TORTILLAS ARE THE MEXICAN EQUIVALENT OF TOASTED SANDWICHES. SERVE THEM AS SOON AS THEY ARE COOKED, OR THEY WILL BECOME CHEWY.

2 Spear the chilli on a long-handled metal skewer and roast it over the flame of a gas burner until the skin blisters and darkens. Do not let the flesh burn. Alternatively, dry-fry it in a griddle pan until the skin is scorched. Place the roasted chilli in a strong plastic bag and tie the top to keep the steam in. Set aside for 20 minutes.

3 Remove the chilli from the bag and peel off the skin. Cut off the stalk, then slit the chilli and scrape out the seeds. Cut the flesh into 8 thin strips.

4 Warm a large frying pan or griddle. Place 1 wheat tortilla on the pan or griddle at a time, sprinkle about one-eighth of the cheese on to 1 half and add a strip of chilli. Fold the tortilla over the cheese and press the edges gently together. Cook the tortilla for 1 minute, then turn over and cook the other side for 1 minute. You can prepare these in advance but cook only when needed.

SERVES FOUR

INGREDIENTS
   200g/7oz mozzarella, Monterey Jack
     or mild Cheddar cheese
   1 fresh fresno chilli
   8 wheat flour tortillas, about
     15cm/6in across
   onion relish or classic tomato salsa,
     to serve

1 If using mozzarella cheese, place it in the freezer for 30 minutes to make it easier to slice. Drain it thoroughly and pat it dry, then slice it into thin strips. Monterey Jack and Cheddar cheese should both be coarsely grated (shredded), as finely grated cheese will melt and ooze away when cooking. Set the cheese aside in a bowl.

5 Remove the filled tortilla from the pan or griddle, cut it into 3 triangles or 4 strips and serve at once, with the onion relish or tomato salsa.

VARIATIONS
Try spreading a thin layer of your favourite Mexican salsa on the tortilla before adding the cheese, or adding a few pieces of cooked chicken before folding the tortilla in half.

Spicy Potato Wedges with Chilli Dip

THESE DRY-ROASTED POTATO WEDGES WITH CRISP SPICY CRUSTS ARE DELICIOUS WITH THE CHILLI DIP.

SERVES TWO

INGREDIENTS
  2 baking potatoes, about 225g/
    8oz each
  30ml/2 tbsp olive oil
  2 garlic cloves, crushed
  5ml/1 tsp ground allspice
  5ml/1 tsp ground coriander
  15ml/1 tbsp paprika
  salt and ground black pepper
For the dip
  15ml/1 tbsp olive oil
  1 small onion, finely chopped
  1 garlic clove, crushed
  200g/7oz can chopped tomatoes
  1 fresh red chilli, seeded and
    finely chopped
  15ml/1 tbsp balsamic vinegar
  15ml/1 tbsp chopped fresh coriander
    (cilantro), plus extra to garnish

1 Preheat the oven to 200°C/400°F/
Gas 6. Cut the potatoes in half, then
into 8 wedges.

2 Add the wedges to a pan of cold
water. Bring to the boil, then reduce the
heat and simmer gently for 10 minutes
or until the wedges have softened
slightly but the flesh has not started to
disintegrate. Drain well and pat dry on
kitchen paper.

COOK'S TIP
To save time, par-boil the potatoes and
toss them with the spices in advance,
but make sure that the potato wedges
are perfectly dry and completely covered
in the spice mixture before roasting.

3 Mix the olive oil, garlic, allspice,
coriander and paprika in a roasting pan.
Add salt and pepper to taste. Add the
potatoes to the pan and shake to coat
them thoroughly. Roast for 20 minutes,
until the wedges are browned, crisp and
fully cooked. Turn the potato wedges
occasionally during the roasting time.

4 Meanwhile, make the chilli dip. Heat
the oil in a small pan, add the onion
and garlic, and cook for 5–10 minutes
until soft.

5 Tip in the chopped tomatoes, with any
juice. Stir in the chilli and vinegar. Cook
gently for 10 minutes until the mixture
has reduced and thickened, then taste
and check the seasoning. Stir in the
chopped fresh coriander.

6 Pile the spicy potato wedges on a
plate, garnish with the extra coriander
and serve with the chilli dip.

VARIATION
Instead of balsamic vinegar, try brown
rice vinegar, which has a mellow flavour.

VERMICELLI <u>WITH</u> SPICY CLAM SAUCE

THERE'S A SUBTLE CHILLI FLAVOUR IN THIS ITALIAN DISH. THE TRICK IS TO USE ENOUGH TO MAKE IT LIVELY, AS HERE, BUT NOT SO MUCH THAT YOU CAN'T TASTE THE CLAMS.

SERVES FOUR

INGREDIENTS

   1kg/2¼lb fresh clams, well scrubbed
   250ml/8fl oz/1 cup dry white wine
   2 garlic cloves, bruised
   1 large handful fresh flat leaf parsley
   30ml/2 tbsp olive oil
   1 small onion, finely chopped
   8 ripe Italian plum tomatoes, peeled,
     seeded and finely chopped
   ½–1 fresh red chilli, seeded and
     finely chopped
   350g/12oz dried vermicelli
   salt and ground black pepper

1 Discard any clams that are open or that do not close when sharply tapped against the work surface.

2 Put the wine, garlic and half the parsley into a pan, then the clams. Cover and bring to the boil. Cook for 5 minutes, shaking the pan.

3 Tip the clams into a large colander set over a bowl and let the liquid drain through. Leave the clams until cool enough to handle, then remove about two-thirds of them from their shells, tipping the clam liquor into the bowl of cooking liquid. Discard any clams that have failed to open. Set both shelled and unshelled clams aside, keeping the unshelled clams warm in a bowl covered with a lid.

4 Heat the olive oil in a pan, add the onion and stir over the heat for about 5 minutes until softened and lightly coloured. Add the tomatoes, then strain in the clam cooking liquid. Stir in the chilli and salt and pepper to taste.

5 Bring to the boil, half-cover the pan and simmer gently for 15–20 minutes. Meanwhile, cook the pasta according to the instructions on the packet. Chop the remaining parsley finely.

6 Add the shelled clams to the tomato sauce, stir well and heat through very gently for 2–3 minutes.

7 Drain the cooked pasta well and tip it into a warmed bowl. Taste the sauce for seasoning, then pour the sauce over the pasta and toss everything together well. Garnish with the reserved unshelled clams, arranging them attractively on top of the pasta. Sprinkle the chopped parsley over the pasta and serve immediately.

BLACK PASTA WITH SQUID SAUCE

ANOTHER SHELLFISH DISH WITH A SUBTLE, RATHER THAN A STRIDENT, CHILLI FLAVOUR. DON'T BE TEMPTED TO OMIT THE CHILLI FLAKES — THE DISH WOULD BE THE POORER FOR THEIR ABSENCE.

SERVES FOUR

INGREDIENTS

    105ml/7 tbsp olive oil
    2 shallots, finely chopped
    3 garlic cloves, crushed
    45ml/3 tbsp chopped fresh parsley
    675g/1½lb cleaned squid, cut into
      rings and rinsed
    150ml/¼ pint/⅔ cup dry white wine
    400g/14oz can chopped tomatoes
    2.5ml/½ tsp dried chilli flakes
      or powder
    450g/1lb squid ink tagliatelle
    salt and ground black pepper

1 Heat the oil in a pan and cook the shallots until pale golden, then add the garlic. When the garlic colours a little, add 30ml/2 tbsp of the parsley, stir, then add the squid and stir again. Cook for 3–4 minutes, then pour in the dry white wine.

2 Simmer for a few seconds, then add the tomatoes and chilli flakes. Season with salt and pepper. Cover and simmer gently for about 1 hour, until the squid is tender. Add more water during the cooking time if necessary.

3 Bring a large pan of lightly salted water to the boil and cook the squid ink tagliatelle, following the instructions on the packet, or until it is *al dente*. Drain and return the pasta to the pan. Add the squid sauce and mix well to coat the tagliatelle evenly. Serve in warmed dishes, sprinkling each portion with the remaining chopped parsley.

COOK'S TIPS
• Tagliatelle flavoured with squid ink looks amazing and tastes deliciously of the sea. Look for it in good Italian delicatessens and better supermarkets.
• If you make your own pasta, you can buy sachets of squid ink from delicatessens.
• If you prepare the squid yourself, you will find the ink sac in the innards.

THREE-COLOUR FISH KEBABS

FOR FOOD TO BE APPETIZING, IT NEEDS TO LOOK AS WELL AS TASTE GOOD, AND THIS DISH, WITH ITS SWEET TOMATO AND CHILLI SALSA, SCORES ON BOTH COUNTS.

SERVES FOUR

INGREDIENTS
  120ml/4fl oz/½ cup olive oil
  finely grated (shredded) rind and
    juice of 1 large lemon
  5ml/1 tsp crushed chilli flakes
  350g/12oz monkfish fillet, cubed
  350g/12oz swordfish fillet, cubed
  350g/12oz thick salmon fillet or
    steak, cubed
  2 red, yellow or orange (bell)
    peppers, cored, seeded and cut
    into squares
  30ml/2 tbsp finely chopped fresh flat
    leaf parsley
  salt and ground black pepper
For the salsa
  2 ripe tomatoes, finely chopped
  1 garlic clove, crushed
  1 fresh red chilli, seeded
    and chopped
  45ml/3 tbsp extra virgin olive oil
  15ml/1 tbsp lemon juice
  15ml/1 tbsp finely chopped fresh flat
    leaf parsley
  pinch of granulated sugar

1 Put the oil in a shallow glass or china bowl and add the lemon rind and juice, the chilli flakes and pepper to taste. Whisk to combine, then add the fish chunks. Turn to coat evenly.

2 Add the pepper squares, stir, then cover and marinate in a cool place for 1 hour, turning occasionally. Preheat the grill (broiler) or prepare the barbecue.

COOK'S TIP
Don't let the fish marinate for more than an hour. The lemon juice will start to break down the fibres of the fish after this time and it will be quickly overcooked.

3 Drain the fish and peppers, reserving the marinade, then thread them on to 8 oiled metal skewers. Barbecue or grill (broil) the skewered fish for 5–8 minutes, turning once to ensure even cooking.

4 Meanwhile, make the salsa by mixing all the ingredients in a bowl, seasoning to taste with salt and pepper. Heat the reserved marinade in a small pan, remove from the heat and stir in the parsley, with salt and pepper to taste. Serve the fish kebabs hot, with the marinade spooned over, accompanied by the tomato and chilli salsa.

CHICKEN SATAY

CONCERTINAS OF TENDER CHICKEN, SERVED WITH A CHILLI-FLAVOURED PEANUT SAUCE, ARE IRRESISTIBLE. GARNISH WITH SLICED FRESH RED CHILLIES FOR EXTRA FIRE.

SERVES FOUR

INGREDIENTS

    4 boneless, skinless chicken
      breast portions
    10ml/2 tsp soft light brown sugar
For the marinade
    5ml/1 tsp cumin seeds
    5ml/1 tsp fennel seeds
    7.5ml/1½ tsp coriander seeds
    6 small onions, chopped
    1 garlic clove, crushed
    1 lemon grass stalk, trimmed
    3 macadamia nuts or 6 cashew nuts
    2.5ml/½ tsp ground turmeric
For the peanut sauce
    4 small onions, sliced
    2 garlic cloves, crushed
    1cm/½in cube shrimp paste
    6 cashew nuts or almonds
    2 lemon grass stalks, trimmed, lower
      5cm/2in sliced
    45ml/3 tbsp sunflower oil, plus extra
    5–10ml/1–2 tsp chilli powder
    400ml/14fl oz can coconut milk
    60–75ml/4–5 tbsp tamarind water or
      30ml/2 tbsp tamarind concentrate
      mixed with 45ml/3 tbsp water
    15ml/1 tbsp soft light brown sugar
    175g/6oz/½ cup crunchy peanut butter

1 Cut the chicken into 16 thin strips, sprinkle with the sugar and set aside.

2 Make the marinade. Dry-fry the spices, then grind to a powder in a food processor. Set aside. Add the onions and garlic to the processor. Chop the lower 5cm/2in of the lemon grass and add with the nuts, spices and turmeric. Grind to a paste; scrape into a bowl.

3 Add the chicken and stir well until coated. Cover loosely with clear film (plastic wrap) and leave to marinate for at least 4 hours. Soak 16 bamboo skewers for 1 hour in a bowl of warm water before use to prevent scorching.

4 Prepare the sauce. Pound or process the onions with the garlic and shrimp paste. Add the nuts and the lower parts of the lemon grass stalks. Process to a fine purée. Heat the oil in a wok and fry the purée for 2–3 minutes. Add the chilli powder and cook for 2 minutes more.

5 Stir in the coconut milk and bring slowly to the boil. Reduce the heat and stir in the tamarind water and brown sugar. Add the peanut butter and cook over a low heat, stirring gently, until fairly thick. Keep warm. Prepare the barbecue or preheat the grill (broiler).

6 Thread the chicken on to the bamboo skewers. Cook on the barbecue or under the grill for about 5 minutes or until golden and tender, brushing with oil occasionally. Serve with the hot peanut sauce handed around in a separate bowl.

CHICKEN FLAUTAS WITH FRESNO CHILLI SALSA

CRISP FRIED TORTILLAS WITH A CHICKEN AND CHEESE FILLING MAKE A DELICIOUS LIGHT MEAL, ESPECIALLY WHEN SERVED WITH A SPICY TOMATO SALSA.

MAKES TWELVE

INGREDIENTS
2 skinless, boneless chicken
  breast portions
15ml/1 tbsp vegetable oil
1 onion, chopped
2 garlic cloves, crushed
90g/3½oz/generous ½ cup crumbled
  feta cheese
12 corn tortillas
oil, for frying
salt and ground black pepper
For the salsa
  3 tomatoes, peeled seeded
    and chopped
  juice of ½ lime
  small bunch of fresh coriander
    (cilantro), chopped
  ½ small onion, finely chopped
  3 fresh green fresno chillies or
    similar fresh green chillies, seeded
    and chopped

1 Start by making the salsa. Mix the chopped tomatoes, lime juice, chopped coriander, onion and chillies in a bowl. Season with salt to taste, cover and chill until needed.

COOK'S TIP
When it comes to cooking the flutes, you might find it easier to keep the cocktail sticks or toothpicks in place until after the flutes have been fried. Remove them before serving.

2 Put the chicken portions in a large pan, add water to cover and bring to the boil. Reduce the heat and simmer for 15–20 minutes or until the chicken is cooked. Remove the chicken from the pan and let it cool a little. Using 2 forks, shred the chicken into small pieces. Set it aside.

3 Heat the oil in a frying pan and fry the onion and garlic over a low heat for about 5 minutes, or until the onion has softened but not coloured. Add the shredded chicken, with salt and pepper to taste. Mix well, remove from the heat and stir in the feta.

4 Before attempting to roll the tortillas, soften 3 or 4 at a time by steaming them on a plate over boiling water. Alternatively, wrap them in microwave-safe clear film (plastic wrap) and then heat them in a microwave oven on full power for about 30 seconds.

5 Place a teaspoonful of the chicken filling on one of the tortillas. Roll the tortilla tightly around the filling to make a neat cylinder. Secure with a cocktail stick or toothpick. Immediately cover the roll with clear film to prevent the tortilla from drying out and splitting. Fill and roll the remaining tortillas in exactly the same way, covering them each time with clear film.

6 Pour oil into a frying pan to a depth of 2.5cm/1in. Heat it until a small cube of day-old bread, added to the oil, rises to the surface and bubbles at the edges before turning golden. Remove the cocktail sticks or toothpicks, then add the flutes to the pan, a few at a time.

7 Fry the flutes for 2–3 minutes until golden, turning frequently. Drain on kitchen paper and serve at once, with the spicy tomato salsa.

TORTAS

FILLED ROLLS WITH A DIFFERENCE, TORTAS ARE LIKE EDIBLE TREASURE CHESTS, WITH MEAT, CHEESE, CHILLIES AND TOMATOES PILED ON TOP OF REFRIED BEANS.

SERVES TWO

INGREDIENTS
    2 fresh jalapeño chillies
    juice of ½ lime
    2 French bread rolls or 2 pieces of
        French bread
    115g/4oz/⅔ cup home-made or
        canned refried beans
    150g/5oz roast pork
    2 small tomatoes, sliced
    115g/4oz Cheddar cheese, sliced
    small bunch of fresh
        coriander (cilantro)
    30ml/2 tbsp crème fraîche

VARIATIONS
The essential ingredients of a *torta* are refried beans and chillies. Everything else is subject to change. Ham, chicken or turkey could all be used instead of pork, or another kind of cheese, and lettuce is often added.

1 Cut the chillies in half, scrape out the seeds, then cut the flesh into thin strips. Put it in a bowl, pour over the lime juice and leave to stand.

2 If using rolls, slice them in half and remove some of the crumb so that they are slightly hollowed. If using French bread, slice each piece in half lengthways and hollow likewise. Set the tops aside and spread the bottom halves with the refried beans.

3 Cut the pork into thin shreds and put these on top of the refried beans. Top with the tomato slices. Drain the jalapeño strips and put them on top of the tomato slices. Add the cheese and sprinkle with coriander leaves.

4 Turn the top halves of the bread or rolls over, so that the cut sides are uppermost, and spread these with crème fraîche. Sandwich back together again and serve.

LIVELY LAMB BURGERS WITH CHILLI RELISH

A RED ONION RELISH SPIKED WITH CHILLI WORKS WELL WITH BURGERS. BASED ON MIDDLE-EASTERN-STYLE LAMB THESE CAN BE SERVED WITH PITTA BREAD AND TABBOULEH OR WITH FRIES AND A SALAD.

SERVES FOUR

INGREDIENTS
  25g/1oz/3 tbsp bulgur wheat
  150ml/¼ pint/⅔ cup hot water
  500g/1¼lb lean minced
    (ground) lamb
  1 small red onion, finely chopped
  2 garlic cloves, finely chopped
  1 fresh green chilli, seeded and
    finely chopped
  5ml/1 tsp ground toasted
    cumin seeds
  5ml/1 tsp grated lemon rind
  60ml/4 tbsp chopped fresh flat
    leaf parsley
  30ml/2 tbsp chopped fresh mint
  olive oil, for frying
  salt and ground black pepper
For the relish
  2 red (bell) peppers, halved
    and seeded
  2 red onions, sliced into wedges
  75–90ml/5–6 tbsp extra virgin olive
    oil
  350g/12oz cherry tomatoes, chopped
  1 fresh red or green chilli, seeded
    and finely chopped
  30ml/2 tbsp chopped fresh mint
  30ml/2 tbsp chopped fresh parsley
  15ml/1 tbsp chopped fresh oregano
    or marjoram
  2.5–5ml/½–1 tsp ground toasted
    cumin seeds
  5ml/1 tsp grated (shredded)
    lemon rind
  juice of ½ lemon
  granulated sugar

1 Put the bulgur wheat in a bowl and pour over the hot water. Leave to stand for 15 minutes. Tip into a colander lined with a clean dishtowel. Drain well, then gather up the sides of the towel and squeeze out the excess moisture.

2 Place the bulgur in a bowl and add the lamb, onion, garlic, chilli, cumin, lemon rind, parsley and mint. Mix well, season, then form the mixture into 8 small burgers. Set aside while you make the relish.

3 Grill (broil) the peppers, skin-side up, until the skin chars and blisters. Place in a strong plastic bag and tie the top to keep the steam in. Set aside for about 20 minutes, then remove the peppers from the bag, peel off the skins and dice the flesh finely. Put the diced pepper in a bowl.

4 Meanwhile, brush the onions with 15ml/1 tbsp of the oil and grill for about 5 minutes on each side, until browned. Cool, then chop. Add to the peppers.

5 Add tomatoes, chilli, mint, parsley, oregano or marjoram and the cumin. Stir in 60ml/4 tbsp of the remaining oil, with the lemon rind and juice. Season with salt, pepper and sugar and allow to stand for 20–30 minutes for the flavours to mature.

6 Heat a heavy frying pan or a ridged cast-iron griddle pan over a high heat and grease lightly with oil. Cook the burgers for about 5–6 minutes on each side, or until just cooked at the centre.

7 While the burgers are cooking, taste the relish and adjust the seasoning. Serve the burgers immediately they are cooked, with the relish.

COOK'S TIP
Oregano (*Origanum vulgare*) is also known as wild marjoram. It has a spicier flavour than marjoram (which is also known as sweet marjoram).

Chillies need to be used judiciously with fish and
shellfish if they are not to overwhelm the flavour of
these ocean ingredients, but where the fish are robust the
results can be superb. Net plenty of compliments by
serving Fiery Fish Stew or Seared Tuna with Red
Onion Salsa. For tenderness and warmth, try Squid and
Chilli Risotto or Thai Fried Noodles.

Fish and Shellfish

FIERY FISH STEW

CHILLI POWDER AND FRESH CHILLIES ARE USED IN THIS SPICY DISH, SO THERE'S DOUBLE DELIGHT FOR ANYONE WHO LIKES THEIR FOOD GOOD AND HOT.

2 Stir in the salt, ground cumin, ground coriander and chilli powder, and cook for 3–4 minutes.

3 Add the tomatoes and potatoes, then stir in the fish stock. Bring to the boil, then reduce the heat and simmer for 10 minutes.

SERVES FOUR

INGREDIENTS

   30ml/2 tbsp oil
   5ml/1 tsp cumin seeds
   1 onion, chopped
   1 red (bell) pepper, thinly sliced
   1 garlic clove, crushed
   2 fresh red chillies, finely chopped
   2 bay leaves
   2.5ml/½ tsp salt
   5ml/1 tsp ground cumin
   5ml/1 tsp ground coriander
   5ml/1 tsp chilli powder
   400g/14oz can chopped tomatoes
   2 large potatoes, cut into 2.5cm/
     1in chunks
   300ml/½ pint/1¼ cups fish stock
   4 cod fillets
   chapatis, to serve

1 Heat the oil in a large, deep-sided frying pan and fry the cumin seeds for 2 minutes until they begin to splutter. (You may need to cover the pan at this stage to prevent the seeds from leaping out, but do not let them burn.) Add the onion, pepper, garlic, chillies and bay leaves, and fry for 5–7 minutes until the onions have browned.

4 Add the fish, then cover and simmer for 10 minutes, or until the fish is tender. Serve with the chapatis.

COOK'S TIP
The potatoes will help to moderate the heat of this curry, but if you prefer a milder flavour, use half the amount of fresh chillies and a mild chilli powder.

BALINESE FISH CURRY

A SIMPLE FISH CURRY IS THE IDEAL DISH TO PREPARE WHEN YOU DON'T HAVE A GREAT DEAL OF TIME.
THE CURRY SAUCE CAN BE MADE IN ADVANCE, AND THE FISH TAKES ONLY MINUTES TO COOK.

SERVES FOUR TO SIX

INGREDIENTS

675g/1½lb cod or haddock fillet
celery leaves or chopped fresh chilli,
   to garnish
boiled rice, to serve

For the sauce

1cm/½in cube shrimp paste
2 red or white onions
2.5cm/1in fresh root ginger, peeled
   and sliced
1cm/½in fresh galangal, peeled
   and sliced
2 garlic cloves
1–2 fresh red chillies, seeded
   and sliced
90ml/6 tbsp sunflower oil
15ml/1 tbsp dark soy sauce
5ml/1 tsp tamarind pulp, soaked in
   30ml/2 tbsp warm water
   then strained
250ml/8fl oz/1 cup water

1 Skin the fish, remove any bones with a pair of tweezers, and then cut the flesh into bitesize pieces. Pat dry with kitchen paper and set aside.

2 Grind the shrimp paste, onions, ginger, galangal, garlic and fresh chillies to a paste in a food processor or with a mortar and pestle.

VARIATIONS
• Use 450g/1lb cooked tiger prawns (jumbo shrimp) instead of fish. Add them 3 minutes before the end of the cooking time.
• If you don't have any fresh chillies, use 5–10ml/1–2 tsp chilli powder.

3 Heat 30ml/2 tbsp of the oil in a pan and fry the spices, stirring, for about 2 minutes. Add the soy sauce and the tamarind liquid, with the water. Cook for 2–3 minutes, stirring.

4 Heat the remaining oil in a separate pan and fry the fish for 2–3 minutes. Turn once only so that the pieces stay whole. Lift out with a slotted spoon and put into the sauce.

5 Cook the fish in the sauce for 3 minutes, until cooked through. Spoon on to a serving dish, garnish with feathery celery leaves or a little chopped fresh chilli and serve with the rice.

COOK'S TIPS
• Save time by asking the fishmonger to skin the fish for you.
• Tamarind has a refreshing acid taste.

COCONUT SALMON

CHILLIES AND COCONUT MILK HAVE A SPECIAL AFFINITY, THE FORMER FURNISHING FIRE WHILE THE LATTER IS COOL AND CREAMY. THIS DELECTABLE DISH CAN BE MADE IN NEXT TO NO TIME.

SERVES FOUR

INGREDIENTS
  10ml/2 tsp ground cumin
  10ml/2 tsp chilli powder
  2.5ml/½ tsp ground turmeric
  30ml/2 tbsp white wine vinegar
  1.5ml/¼ tsp salt
  4 salmon steaks, about
    175g/6oz each
  45ml/3 tbsp oil
  1 onion, chopped
  2 fresh green chillies, seeded
    and chopped
  2 garlic cloves, crushed
  2.5cm/1in piece root ginger,
    grated (shredded)
  5ml/1 tsp ground coriander
  175ml/6fl oz/¾ cup coconut milk
  spring onion (scallion) rice, to serve
  fresh coriander (cilantro) sprigs,
    to garnish

1 In a small bowl, mix half the cumin with the chilli powder, turmeric, vinegar and salt. Place the salmon in a single layer in a non-metallic dish and rub all over with the paste. Cover and leave to marinate for 15 minutes.

COOK'S TIP
Make coconut milk by dissolving grated (shredded) creamed coconut (coconut cream) in boiling water, then strain.

2 Heat the oil in a wide, deep-sided frying pan and fry the onion, chillies, garlic and ginger for 5–6 minutes. Scrape the mixture into a food processor or blender and process to a paste. Use a hand-held blender if you prefer.

3 Return the paste to the pan. Add the coriander and remaining cumin, then pour in the coconut milk, stirring constantly. Bring to the boil, then simmer for 5 minutes.

4 Add the salmon steaks and spoon the sauce over them. Cover and cook for 15 minutes until the fish is tender. Serve with spring onion rice and garnish with coriander sprigs.

SALMON WITH TEQUILA CREAM SAUCE

ROASTED JALAPEÑO CHILLIES AND LIGHTLY AGED REPOSADA TEQUILA ARE A WINNING COMBINATION.
THIS EXCITING AND UNUSUAL FISH DISH IS PERFECT FOR A DINNER PARTY.

SERVES FOUR

INGREDIENTS

3 fresh green jalapeño chillies
45ml/3 tbsp olive oil
1 small onion, finely chopped
150ml/¼ pint/⅔ cup fish stock
grated (shredded) rind and juice
 of 1 lime
120ml/4fl oz/½ cup single
 (light) cream
30ml/2 tbsp reposada tequila
1 firm avocado
4 salmon fillets
salt and ground white pepper
strips of green (bell) pepper and
 fresh flat leaf parsley, to garnish

3 Stir the cream into the onion and
stock mixture. Slice the chilli flesh into
strips and add to the pan. Cook over a
gentle heat, stirring constantly, for
2–3 minutes. Season to taste with salt
and white pepper.

4 Stir the tequila into the onion and
chilli mixture. Leave the pan over a very
low heat. Peel the avocado, remove the
stone (pit) and slice the flesh. Brush
the salmon fillets on one side with a
little of the remaining oil.

5 Heat a frying pan or ridged griddle
pan until very hot and add the salmon,
oiled side down. Cook for 2–3 minutes,
until the underside is golden, then
brush the top with oil, turn each fillet
over and cook the other side until the
fish is cooked and flakes easily when
tested with the tip of a sharp knife.

6 Serve on a pool of sauce, with the
avocado slices. Garnish with strips of
green pepper and fresh parsley. This
dish is good with fried potatoes.

1 Roast the chillies in a frying pan until
the skins are blistered but not burnt.
Put them in a strong plastic bag and tie
the top to keep the steam in. Set aside.

2 Heat 15ml/1 tbsp of the oil in a pan.
Add the onion and fry for 3–4 minutes,
then pour in the stock with the lime rind
and juice. Cook for 10 minutes, until
the stock starts to reduce. Remove the
chillies from the bag. Peel them, then
slit and scrape out the seeds.

SPICED FISH WITH CHILLIES, LEMON AND RED ONIONS

SOMETIMES IT'S THE SIMPLEST DISHES THAT MAKE THE MOST IMPACT. THIS DISH NOT ONLY LOOKS PRETTY, IT ALSO TASTES GOOD, WITH PAPRIKA AND FRESH RED CHILLIES GIVING IT CHARACTER.

SERVES FOUR

INGREDIENTS

4 halibut or cod steaks or cutlets, about 175g/6oz each
juice of 1 lemon
5ml/1 tsp crushed garlic
5ml/1 tsp paprika
5ml/1 tsp ground cumin
4ml/¾ tsp dried tarragon
about 60ml/4 tbsp olive oil, plus extra for frying the onion
flour, for dusting
300ml/½ pint/1¼ cups fish stock
2 fresh red chillies, seeded and finely chopped
30ml/2 tbsp chopped fresh coriander (cilantro)
1 red onion, cut into rings
salt and ground black pepper

1 Place the fish in a single layer in a shallow dish. Mix together the lemon juice, garlic, paprika, cumin, tarragon and a little salt and pepper. Spoon over the fish, cover loosely with clear film (plastic wrap) and marinate for a few hours or overnight in the refrigerator. The longer the fish is left to marinate, the stronger the flavour will be.

2 Gently heat the olive oil in a large non-stick frying pan. Drain the fish, dust the pieces with flour, then fry for a few minutes on each side, until golden brown all over.

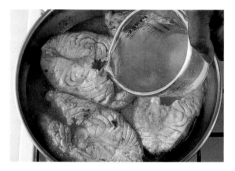

3 Pour the fish stock around the fish, and simmer, covered, for about 5 minutes until the fish is thoroughly cooked through.

4 Add the chopped red chillies and 15ml/1 tbsp of the coriander to the pan. Simmer for 5 minutes.

5 Transfer the fish and sauce to a serving plate and keep warm.

6 Wipe the pan, heat some extra olive oil and stir-fry the onion rings until speckled brown. Arrange them over the fish, with the remaining chopped coriander and serve at once.

RED SNAPPER WITH CHILLI, GIN AND GINGER SAUCE

CHILLIES, GINGER AND GIN ADD SPICE AND PIQUANCY TO A COLOURFUL FISH DISH THAT TASTES EVERY BIT AS GOOD AS IT LOOKS. BAKED IN THE OVEN, IT IS IDEAL FOR ENTERTAINING.

SERVES FOUR

INGREDIENTS
1 red snapper, about
  1.6kg/3½lb, cleaned
30ml/2 tbsp sunflower oil
1 onion, chopped
2 garlic cloves, crushed
50g/2oz/½ cup sliced button
  (white) mushrooms
5ml/1 tsp ground coriander
15ml/1 tbsp chopped fresh parsley
30ml/2 tbsp grated (shredded) fresh
  root ginger
2 fresh red chillies, seeded
  and sliced
15ml/1 tbsp cornflour (cornstarch)
45ml/3 tbsp gin
300ml/½ pint/1¼ cups chicken or
  vegetable stock
salt and ground black pepper
For the garnish
15ml/1 tbsp sunflower oil
6 garlic cloves, sliced
1 lettuce heart, finely shredded
1 bunch fresh coriander (cilantro),
  tied with red raffia

1 Preheat the oven to 190°C/375°F/ Gas 5. Grease a flameproof dish that is large enough to hold the fish. Make several diagonal cuts on one side of the fish.

2 Heat the oil in a frying pan and gently fry the onion, garlic and sliced mushrooms for 2–3 minutes. Stir in the ground coriander and the chopped parsley. Season with salt and pepper to taste.

3 Spoon the filling into the cavity of the fish, then lift the snapper into the dish. Pour in enough cold water to cover the base of the dish. Sprinkle the ginger and chillies over, then cover and bake for 30–40 minutes, basting from time to time. Remove the cover for the last 10 minutes.

4 Carefully lift the snapper on to a serving dish, cover with foil and keep hot. Tip the cooking juices from the dish into a pan.

5 Mix the cornflour and gin in a cup and stir into the cooking juices. Pour in the stock. Bring to the boil and cook gently for 3–4 minutes or until thickened, stirring. Taste for seasoning, then pour into a bowl.

6 Make the garnish. Heat the oil in a small pan and stir-fry the garlic and lettuce over a high heat until crisp. Spoon alongside the snapper. Place the coriander bouquet on the other side. Serve with the sauce.

SEARED TUNA WITH RED ONION SALSA

A FRUITY CHILLI SUCH AS ITALIA WOULD BE GOOD IN THIS SALSA, AS WOULD A PEACHY POBLANO CHILLI. THE SALSA MAKES A FINE ACCOMPANIMENT FOR THE TUNA.

SERVES FOUR

INGREDIENTS

    4 tuna loin steaks, each weighing
      about 175–200g/6–7oz
    5ml/1 tsp cumin seeds, toasted
      and crushed
    pinch of dried red chilli flakes
    grated (shredded) rind and juice
      of 1 lime
    45–60ml/3–4 tbsp extra virgin
      olive oil
    salt and ground black pepper
    lime wedges and coriander (cilantro)
      sprigs, to garnish
For the salsa
    1 small red onion, finely chopped
    6 red or yellow cherry tomatoes,
      roughly chopped
    1 avocado, peeled, stoned (pitted)
      and chopped
    2 kiwi fruit, peeled and chopped
    1 fresh red or green chilli, seeded
      and finely chopped
    60ml/4 tbsp chopped fresh
      coriander (cilantro)
    leaves from 6 fresh mint sprigs,
      finely chopped
    5–10ml/1–2 tsp Thai fish sauce
      (*nam pla*)
    about 5ml/1 tsp muscovado
      (molasses) sugar

1 Wash the tuna steaks and pat them dry with kitchen paper. Sprinkle with half the crushed cumin seeds, the dried chilli flakes, a little salt and freshly ground black pepper and half the lime rind and juice. Rub in 30ml/ 2 tbsp of the olive oil and set aside in a glass or china dish for 30 minutes.

2 Meanwhile, make the salsa: mix the onion, tomatoes, avocado, kiwi fruit, fresh chilli, chopped coriander and mint in a bowl. Add the remaining crushed cumin, the rest of the lime rind and half the remaining lime juice. Add Thai fish sauce and sugar to taste. Set aside for 15–20 minutes for the flavours to develop, then add a further seasoning of Thai fish sauce, lime juice and olive oil to taste.

3 Heat a ridged, cast-iron grill (broiling) pan for at least 5 minutes. Cook the tuna, allowing about 3 minutes on each side if you like it rare or a little longer for a medium result.

4 Serve the tuna steaks immediately, garnished with lime wedges and coriander sprigs. Serve the salsa separately or spoon some or all of it on the plates with the tuna.

STIR-FRIED PRAWNS ON CRISP NOODLE CAKE

THE CONTRAST BETWEEN THE CRISP NOODLE CAKE AND THE SUCCULENT VEGETABLES AND SHELLFISH WORKS EXTREMELY WELL, AND THE CHILLI RINGS ADD COLOUR AND A FINAL BURST OF HEAT.

SERVES FOUR

INGREDIENTS

    300g/11oz thin dried egg noodles
    60ml/4 tbsp vegetable oil
    500g/1¼lb medium raw king
      prawns (jumbo shrimp), peeled
      and deveined
    2.5ml/½ tsp ground coriander
    15ml/1 tbsp ground turmeric
    2 garlic cloves, finely chopped
    2 slices fresh root ginger,
      finely chopped
    tender parts of 2 lemon grass stalks,
      finely chopped
    2 shallots, finely chopped
    15ml/1 tbsp tomato purée (paste)
    250ml/8fl oz/1 cup coconut milk
    15–30ml/1–2 tbsp lime juice
    15–30ml/1–2 tbsp Thai fish sauce
      (*nam pla*)
    1 cucumber, peeled, seeded and cut
      into 5cm/2in batons
    4–6 fresh kaffir lime leaves (optional)
    1 tomato, seeded and cut into strips
    2 fresh red chillies, seeded and
      finely sliced in rings
    salt and ground black pepper
    2 spring onions (scallions), finely
      sliced, and a few coriander
      (cilantro) sprigs, to garnish

1 Bring a pan of lightly salted water to the boil, add the egg noodles and remove the pan from the heat. Cover and set aside for about 10 minutes, until just tender. Drain, rinse under cold running water and drain again well.

COOK'S TIPS
• Any red chillies can be used here, but you would be wise to avoid incendiary varieties like habanero or Scotch bonnet. Red fresno chillies, red serranos or even a mild red wax chilli would be suitable.
• You can, of course, use fresh noodles for this dish. It is always worth buying them if you can, because they can be frozen and then used as needed. They defrost quickly when dropped in boiling water.

2 Heat 15ml/1 tbsp of the oil in a large frying pan. Add the noodles in an even layer and fry for 4–5 minutes until they form a crisp, golden cake. Turn the noodle cake over and fry the other side. Alternatively, make 4 individual cakes. Keep hot.

3 In a bowl, toss the prawns with the ground coriander, turmeric, garlic, ginger and lemon grass. Add salt and pepper to taste.

4 Heat the remaining oil in a large frying pan. Fry the shallots for 1 minute, then add the prawns and fry for 2 minutes more. Using a slotted spoon, remove the prawns.

5 Stir the tomato purée and coconut milk into the mixture remaining in the pan. Stir in lime juice to taste and season with the fish sauce. Bring the sauce to a simmer, gently stir in the prawns, then add the cucumber and the kaffir lime leaves, if using. Simmer gently until the prawns are cooked and the sauce has reduced to a nice coating consistency.

6 Add the tomato, stir until just warmed through, then add the chillies. Serve the prawns in the sauce on top of the crisp noodle cake(s), and garnish with the sliced spring onions and coriander sprigs.

SQUID AND CHILLI RISOTTO

SQUID NEEDS TO BE COOKED VERY QUICKLY OR VERY SLOWLY. HERE THE SQUID IS MARINATED IN LIME AND KIWI FRUIT — A POPULAR METHOD IN NEW ZEALAND FOR TENDERIZING SQUID.

SERVES THREE TO FOUR

INGREDIENTS
about 450g/1lb squid
about 45ml/3 tbsp olive oil
15g/½oz/1 tbsp butter
1 onion, finely chopped
2 garlic cloves, crushed
1 fresh red chilli, seeded and
   finely sliced
275g/10oz/1½ cups risotto rice
175ml/6fl oz/¾ cup dry white wine
1 litre/1¾ pints/4 cups simmering
   fish stock
30ml/2 tbsp chopped fresh
   coriander (cilantro)
salt and ground black pepper
For the marinade
2 ripe kiwi fruit, chopped
   and mashed
1 fresh red chilli, seeded and
   thinly sliced
30ml/2 tbsp lime juice

1 If not already cleaned, prepare the squid by cutting off the tentacles at the base and pulling to remove the quill. Discard the quill and intestines, if necessary, and pull away the thin outer skin. Rinse the body and cut into thin strips: cut the tentacles into short pieces, discarding both the beak and the eyes.

2 Put the kiwi fruit for the marinade in a bowl, then stir in the chilli and lime juice. Add the squid, stirring to coat all the strips in the mixture. Season with salt and pepper, cover with clear film (plastic wrap) and set aside in the refrigerator for 4 hours or overnight.

3 Drain the squid. Heat 15ml/1 tbsp of the olive oil in a frying pan and cook the strips, in batches if necessary, for about 30–60 seconds over a high heat. It is important that the squid cooks very quickly to keep it tender.

4 Transfer the cooked squid to a plate and set aside. Don't worry if some of the marinade clings to the squid, but if too much juice accumulates in the pan, pour this into a jug and add more olive oil when cooking the next batch, so that the squid fries rather than simmers. Reserve the accumulated juices in a jug.

5 Heat the remaining oil with the butter in a large pan and gently fry the onion and garlic for 5–6 minutes until soft. Add the sliced chilli to the pan and fry for 1 minute more.

COOK'S TIPS
• You can only make a true risotto with Italian risotto rice. Names to look for are Arborio, Carnaroli, Roma and Baldo. These are the rices that give the right kind of creamy texture.
• As in this recipe, always use a well-flavoured stock.

6 Add the rice. Cook for a few minutes, stirring, until the rice is coated with oil and is slightly translucent, then stir in the wine until it has been absorbed.

7 Gradually add the hot stock and the reserved cooking liquid from the squid, a ladleful at a time, stirring the rice constantly and waiting until each quantity of stock has been absorbed before adding the next.

8 When the rice is about three-quarters cooked, stir in the squid and continue cooking the risotto until all the stock has been absorbed and the rice is tender, but retains a bit of "bite". Stir in the chopped coriander, cover with the lid or a dishtowel, and leave to rest for a few minutes before serving.

VARIATIONS
• Use a long hot chilli, such as cayenne, for this dish, or try a milder variety, such as a red fresno.
• You can use a habanero if you like, but one-quarter or half will probably be sufficient, and remember to wear gloves when you handle it.

AROMATIC MUSSEL RISOTTO

FRESH ROOT GINGER ADDS A DISTINCTIVE FLAVOUR TO THIS DISH, WHILE THE GREEN CHILLIES GIVE IT A LITTLE HEAT. USE JALAPEÑOS OR SERRANOS.

SERVES THREE TO FOUR

INGREDIENTS
  900g/2lb live mussels
  about 250ml/8fl oz/1 cup dry
    white wine
  30ml/2 tbsp olive oil
  1 onion, chopped
  2 garlic cloves, crushed
  1–2 fresh green chillies, seeded and
    finely sliced
  2.5cm/1in piece of fresh root
    ginger, grated (shredded)
  275g/10oz/1½ cups risotto rice
  900ml/1½ pints/3¾ cups simmering
    fish stock
  30ml/2 tbsp chopped fresh
    coriander (cilantro)
  30ml/2 tbsp double (heavy) cream
  salt and ground black pepper

1 Scrub the mussels, discarding any that do not close when sharply tapped. Place in a large pan. Add half the wine and bring to the boil. Cover the pan and cook the mussels for 4–5 minutes until they have opened, shaking the pan occasionally. Drain, reserving the liquid and discarding any mussels that have failed to open. Remove most of the mussels from their shells, reserving a few in their shells for decoration. Strain the mussel liquid.

2 Heat the oil and fry the onion and garlic for 3–4 minutes until beginning to soften. Stir in the chillies. Continue to cook over a low heat for 1–2 minutes, stirring frequently, then stir in the grated ginger and fry very gently for 1 minute more.

3 Add the rice and cook over a medium heat for 2 minutes, stirring, until the rice is coated in oil and the grains become translucent.

4 Stir in the reserved cooking liquid from the mussels. When this has been absorbed, add the remaining wine and cook, stirring, until this has been absorbed. Now add the hot fish stock, a little at a time, making sure that each addition has been absorbed before adding the next.

5 When the rice is about three-quarters cooked, stir in the shelled mussels. Add the coriander and season. Continue adding stock to the risotto until it is creamy and the rice is tender but slightly firm in the centre.

6 Remove the risotto from the heat, stir in the cream, cover and leave to rest for a few minutes. Warm a serving dish and spoon in the risotto, garnish with the reserved mussels in their shells, and serve immediately.

CRAB WITH GREEN RICE

THIS IS A POPULAR DISH IN THE WESTERN COASTAL AREAS OF MEXICO. OTHER TYPES OF SHELLFISH CAN BE USED IF YOU PREFER, AND THE DISH ALSO WORKS WELL WITH WARM CORN TORTILLAS.

SERVES FOUR

INGREDIENTS

225g/8oz/generous 1 cup long
   grain white rice
500g/1¼lb/3⅓ cups drained
   canned tomatillos
large bunch of fresh
   coriander (cilantro)
1 onion, roughly chopped
3 poblano or other fresh green
   chillies, seeded and chopped
3 garlic cloves
45ml/3 tbsp olive oil
500g/1¼lb crab meat
300ml/½ pint/1¼ cups fish stock
60ml/4 tbsp dry white wine
salt
sliced spring onions (scallions),
   to garnish

1 Put the rice in a heatproof bowl, pour over boiling water to cover and leave to stand for 20 minutes. Drain thoroughly.

2 Put the tomatillos in a food processor or blender and process until smooth. Chop half the coriander and add to the tomatillo purée, with the onion, chillies and garlic. Process again until the mixture is smooth.

3 Heat the oil in a large pan. Add the rice and fry over a medium heat for 5 minutes, stirring from time to time, until all the oil has been absorbed. Stir occasionally to prevent the rice from sticking.

4 Stir in the tomatillo mixture, with the crab meat, stock and wine. Cover and cook over a low heat for about 20 minutes or until all the liquid has been absorbed. Stir occasionally and add a little more liquid if the rice starts to stick to the pan. Add salt as required, then spoon into a dish and garnish with coriander and the sliced spring onions.

COOK'S TIP
Tomatillos are the edible purplish fruit of a ground cherry.

CHILLI RAVIOLI WITH CRAB

CHILLI PASTA LOOKS AND TASTES SENSATIONAL. ADD A CREAMY CRAB FILLING AND YOU'VE GOT A GREAT TALKING POINT FOR A DINNER PARTY.

SERVES FOUR

INGREDIENTS
   300g/11oz/2¾ cups strong white
     (bread) flour
   5ml/1 tsp salt
   5–10ml/1–2 tsp crushed dried
     red chillies
   3 eggs
   75g/3oz/6 tbsp butter
   juice of 1 lemon
For the filling
   175g/6oz/¾ cup mascarpone cheese
   175g/6oz crab meat
   30ml/2 tbsp finely chopped fresh flat
     leaf parsley
   finely grated (shredded) rind
     of 1 lemon
   pinch of crushed dried chillies
   salt and ground black pepper

1 Put the flour, salt and dried chillies in a food processor. Add 1 egg and pulse until the ingredients are mixed. Switch the processor to maximum speed and add the remaining eggs through the feeder tube. As soon as the mixture forms a dough, transfer it to a clean work surface and knead for 5 minutes, until smooth and elastic. Wrap in clear film (plastic wrap) and leave to rest for 15 minutes.

COOK'S TIPS
• Mascarpone is a very rich Italian cream cheese that can be used for savoury and sweet dishes.
• You can use a mixture of light and dark crab meat for this dish.
• This dish is best served with a crisp green or herb salad.

2 Make the filling. Put the mascarpone in a bowl and mash it with a fork. Add the crab meat, parsley, lemon rind and crushed dried chillies, with salt and pepper to taste. Stir well.

3 Using a pasta machine, roll out one-quarter of the pasta dough into a 90cm–1 metre/36–39in strip. Cut into two 45–50cm/18–20in lengths. With a 6cm/2½in fluted cutter, firmly cut out 8 squares from each strip.

4 Using a teaspoon, put a mound of filling in the centre of half the squares. Brush a little water around the edge of the filled squares, then top with the plain squares and press the edges to seal. For a decorative finish, press the edges with the tines of a fork.

5 Put the ravioli on floured dishtowels, sprinkle lightly with flour and leave to dry while repeating the process with the remaining dough to make 32 ravioli altogether.

6 Bring a large pan of lightly salted water to the boil and cook the ravioli for 4–5 minutes. Meanwhile, melt the butter and lemon juice in a small pan until sizzling.

7 Drain the ravioli and divide them among 4 warmed bowls. Drizzle the lemon butter over the ravioli and serve.

THAI FRIED NOODLES

THE CHILLI FLAVOUR SIMPLY TEASES THE TASTE BUDS IN THIS CLASSIC THAI RECIPE. IT IS MADE WITH RICE NOODLES AND IS CONSIDERED ONE OF THE NATIONAL DISHES OF THAILAND.

SERVES FOUR TO SIX

INGREDIENTS

  350g/12oz rice noodles
  45ml/3 tbsp vegetable oil
  15ml/1 tbsp chopped garlic
  16 raw king prawns (jumbo shrimp),
    shelled, tails left intact
    and deveined
  2 eggs, lightly beaten
  15ml/1 tbsp dried shrimps, rinsed
  30ml/2 tbsp pickled white radish
  50g/2oz fried beancurd (tofu), cut
    into small slivers
  2.5ml/½ tsp dried chilli flakes
  115g/4oz chives, preferably garlic
    chives, cut into 5cm/2in lengths
  225g/8oz/3–4 cups beansprouts
  50g/2oz/½ cup roasted peanuts,
    coarsely ground
  5ml/1 tsp granulated sugar
  15ml/1 tbsp dark soy sauce
  30ml/2 tbsp Thai fish sauce
    (*nam pla*)
  30ml/2 tbsp tamarind or lime juice
  30ml/2 tbsp coriander (cilantro)
    leaves, to garnish
  1 kaffir lime, to garnish

1 Soak the noodles in warm water for 20–30 minutes, then drain.

2 Heat 15ml/1 tbsp of the oil in a wok. Add the garlic and fry until golden. Stir in the prawns and cook for about 1–2 minutes until pink, tossing from time to time. Remove and set aside.

VARIATION
If you are unable to find kaffir limes use the juiciest variety available.

3 Heat another 15ml/1 tbsp of oil in the wok. Add the eggs and tilt the wok to spread them into a thin sheet. Stir to scramble and break the egg into small pieces. Remove from the wok and set aside with the prawns.

4 Heat the remaining oil in the same wok. Add the dried shrimps, pickled radish, beancurd and chilli flakes. Stir briefly. Add the soaked noodles and stir-fry for 5 minutes.

5 Add the chives, half the beansprouts and half the peanuts. Season with the sugar, soy sauce, fish sauce and tamarind or lime juice. Mix well and cook until the noodles are heated through.

6 Return the prawn and egg mixture to the wok and mix with the noodles. Serve immediately, garnished with the rest of the beansprouts, peanuts, the coriander leaves and lime wedges.

There's nothing nicer than coming home to a hot meal, and when the heat is chilli-inspired, the warmth soon reaches from your head to your toes. This sizzling selection includes Chilli con Carne and Madras Curry alongside the aptly named Scorching Chilli Chicken and Fire Fry. Also on the menu are Tandoori Chicken and a new take on Thai Green Beef Curry.

Poultry and Meat Main Meals

SICHUAN CHICKEN WITH KUNG PO SAUCE

THIS RECIPE COMES FROM THE SICHUAN REGION OF WESTERN CHINA, WHERE CHILLIES ARE WIDELY USED. CASHEW NUTS HAVE BECOME A POPULAR INGREDIENT IN CHINESE COOKING.

SERVES THREE

INGREDIENTS
 2 skinless, boneless chicken
   breast portions, total weight
   about 350g/12oz
 1 egg white
 10ml/2 tsp cornflour (cornstarch)
 2.5ml/½ tsp salt
 30ml/2 tbsp yellow salted beans
 15ml/1 tbsp hoisin sauce
 5ml/1 tsp soft light brown sugar
 15ml/1 tbsp rice wine or
   medium-dry sherry
 15ml/1 tbsp wine vinegar
 4 garlic cloves, crushed
 150ml/¼ pint/⅔ cup chicken stock
 45ml/3 tbsp sunflower oil
 2–3 dried red chillies, chopped
 115g/4oz/1 cup roasted cashew nuts
 fresh coriander (cilantro), to garnish

1 Cut the chicken into neat pieces. Lightly whisk the egg white in a dish, whisk in the cornflour and salt, then add the chicken and stir until coated.

2 In a bowl, mash the beans. Stir in the hoisin sauce, brown sugar, rice wine or sherry, vinegar, garlic and stock.

3 Heat a wok, add the oil and stir-fry the chicken for 2 minutes until tender. Lift out the chicken and set aside.

COOK'S TIP
The yellow beans may be too salty for your taste, so if you like, rinse them in water and drain before using them.

4 Heat the oil remaining in the wok and fry the chilli pieces for 1 minute. Return the chicken to the wok and pour in the bean sauce mixture. Bring to the boil, stir in the cashew nuts and heat through. Spoon into a heated serving dish, garnish with the coriander leaves and serve immediately.

CARIBBEAN PEANUT CHICKEN

LIKE COCONUT, PEANUTS AND PEANUT BUTTER GO PARTICULARLY WELL WITH CHILLIES. PEANUT BUTTER MAKES THIS SAUCE GLORIOUSLY RICH AND CREAMY. USE A MEDIUM-HOT CHILLI.

SERVES FOUR

INGREDIENTS

   4 skinless, boneless chicken breast
     portions, cut into thin strips
   225g/8oz/generous 1 cup white long
     grain rice
   15g/½oz/1 tbsp butter, plus extra
     for greasing
   30ml/2 tbsp groundnut (peanut) oil
   1 onion, finely chopped
   2 tomatoes, peeled, seeded
     and chopped
   1 fresh green chilli, seeded
     and sliced
   60ml/4 tbsp smooth peanut butter
   450ml/¾ pint/scant 2 cups
     chicken stock
   lemon juice, to taste
   salt and ground black pepper
   lime wedges and fresh flat leaf
     parsley sprigs, to garnish
For the marinade
   15ml/1 tbsp sunflower oil
   1–2 garlic cloves, crushed
   5ml/1 tsp chopped fresh thyme
   25ml/1½ tbsp medium curry powder
   juice of ½ lemon

1 Mix all the marinade ingredients in a large bowl and stir in the chicken. Cover loosely with clear film (plastic wrap) and set aside in a cool place for 2–3 hours.

COOK'S TIP
If the casserole is not large enough to allow you to toss the rice with the chicken mixture before serving, invert a large, deep plate over the casserole, turn both over and toss the mixture on the plate before serving.

2 Meanwhile, cook the rice in a large pan of lightly salted boiling water until tender. Drain well and turn into a generously buttered casserole.

3 Preheat the oven to 180°C/350°F/ Gas 4. Heat 15ml/1 tbsp of oil with the butter in a flameproof casserole and fry the chicken pieces for 4–5 minutes until evenly brown. Add more oil if necessary.

4 Lift out the chicken and put it on a plate. Add the finely chopped onion to the flameproof casserole and fry for 5–6 minutes until lightly browned, adding more oil if necessary. Stir in the chopped tomatoes and chilli. Cook over a gentle heat for 3–4 minutes, stirring occasionally. Switch off the heat.

5 Mix the peanut butter with the chicken stock. Stir into the tomato and onion mixture, then add the chicken. Stir in the lemon juice, season to taste, then spoon the mixture over the rice in the casserole.

6 Cover the casserole. Cook in the oven for 15–20 minutes or until piping hot. Use a large spoon to toss the rice with the chicken mixture. Serve at once, garnished with the lime and parsley.

SCORCHING CHILLI CHICKEN

NOT FOR THE FAINT-HEARTED, THIS FIERY, HOT CURRY IS MADE WITH A SPICY CHILLI MASALA PASTE, WHICH IS BLENDED INTO A FRAGRANT SAUCE.

SERVES FOUR

INGREDIENTS
   8 chicken thighs, skinned
   5ml/1 tsp garam masala
   sliced green chillies, to garnish
   chapatis and natural (plain) yogurt,
     to serve
For the paste
   30ml/2 tbsp tomato purée (paste)
   2 garlic cloves, roughly chopped
   2 fresh green chillies, roughly chopped
   5 dried red chillies
   2.5ml/½ tsp salt
   1.5ml/¼ tsp granulated sugar
   5ml/1 tsp chilli powder
   2.5ml/½ tsp paprika
   15ml/1 tbsp curry paste
For the sauce
   30ml/2 tbsp oil
   2.5ml/½ tsp cumin seeds
   1 onion, finely chopped
   2 bay leaves
   5ml/1 tsp ground coriander
   5ml/1 tsp ground cumin
   1.5ml/¼ tsp ground turmeric
   400g/14oz can chopped tomatoes
   150ml/¼ pint/⅔ cup water

1 Put the tomato purée, garlic, fresh green and dried red chillies, salt, sugar, chilli powder, paprika and curry paste into a blender and process until smooth.

2 Heat the oil in a large pan and fry the cumin seeds for 2 minutes. Add the onion and bay, and fry for 5 minutes.

COOK'S TIP
For a milder, fruitier finish, use large red chillies.

3 Stir in the chilli paste and fry for 2–3 minutes, then add the spices. Cook for 2 minutes. Add the tomatoes and water. Bring to the boil. Simmer for 5 minutes until the sauce thickens.

4 Add the chicken and garam masala. Cover and simmer for 25–30 minutes until the chicken is tender. Serve with chapatis and yogurt, garnished with sliced green chillies.

TANDOORI CHICKEN

THIS CLASSIC INDIAN DISH HAS A UNIQUE FLAVOUR. THE CHILLI DOESN'T DOMINATE THE OTHER SPICES, BUT IS NONETHELESS AN ESSENTIAL INGREDIENT.

SERVES FOUR

INGREDIENTS

   8 chicken pieces, such as
     thighs, drumsticks or halved breast
     portions, skinned
   60ml/4 tbsp lemon juice
   10ml/2 tsp salt
   175ml/6fl oz/¾ cup natural
     (plain) yogurt
   5ml/1 tsp chilli powder
   5ml/1 tsp garam masala
   5ml/1 tsp ground cumin
   5ml/1 tsp ground coriander
   2 garlic cloves,
     roughly chopped
   2.5cm/1in piece fresh root ginger,
     roughly chopped
   2 fresh green chillies,
     roughly chopped
   red food colouring (optional)
   25g/1oz/2 tbsp butter, melted
   lemon wedges, salad and cucumber
     raita (see Cook's Tip), to serve
   chopped fresh green chilli or chilli
     powder and a sprig of fresh mint,
     to garnish the raita

1 Cut deep slashes in the chicken pieces. Mix together the lemon juice and half the salt and rub over the chicken. Set aside for 10 minutes.

2 Mix the natural yogurt, the remaining salt, chilli powder, garam masala, ground cumin and ground coriander in a bowl. Put the garlic, ginger and chillies into a food processor or blender and process until smooth. Scrape out of the processor bowl and stir the mixture into the spiced yogurt.

3 Brush the chicken pieces with food colouring, if using, and put them into a dish that is large enough to hold them in a single layer. Spoon over the marinade, turn the pieces until evenly coated, then cover and chill overnight.

4 Preheat the oven to 220°C/425°F/ Gas 7. Put the chicken in a roasting pan and bake for 40 minutes, basting with the melted butter. Serve on a bed of salad, with lemon wedges for squeezing. Offer the raita separately.

COOK'S TIP
Cucumber raita is a wonderfully refreshing dish to serve with anything spicy. To make it, dice 1 cucumber and place it in a bowl. Stir in 300ml/½ pint/ 1¼ cups natural (plain) yogurt, 1.5ml/ ¼ tsp salt and 1.5ml/¼ tsp ground cumin. A chopped fresh green chilli can be added if you like, or top the raita with a dusting of chilli powder and a fresh mint sprig.

TURKEY MOLE

A MOLE IS A RICH STEW, SERVED ON FESTIVE OCCASIONS IN MEXICO. TOASTED NUTS, FRUIT AND CHOCOLATE ARE AMONG THE CLASSIC INGREDIENTS; THIS VERSION INCLUDES COCOA POWDER.

SERVES FOUR

INGREDIENTS
1 ancho chilli, seeded
1 guajillo chilli, seeded
115g/4oz/¾ cup sesame seeds
50g/2oz/½ cup whole
   blanched almonds
50g/2oz/½ cup shelled unsalted
   peanuts, skinned
50g/2oz/¼ cup lard (shortening) or
   60ml/4 tbsp vegetable oil
1 small onion, finely chopped
2 garlic cloves, crushed
50g/2oz/⅓ cup canned tomatoes in
   tomato juice
1 ripe plaintain
50g/2oz/⅓ cup raisins
75g/3oz/½ cup ready-to-eat
   pitted prunes
5ml/1 tsp dried oregano
2.5ml/½ tsp ground cloves
2.5ml/½ tsp crushed allspice berries
5ml/1 tsp ground cinnamon
25g/1oz/¼ cup cocoa powder
4 turkey breast steaks
chopped fresh oregano, to garnish

1 Soak both types of dried chilli in a bowl of hot water for 20–30 minutes, then lift them out and chop them roughly. Reserve 250ml/8fl oz/1 cup of the soaking liquid.

COOK'S TIPS
• It is important to use good-quality cocoa powder, which is unsweetened.
• Mexican-style cocoa powder is available from specialist food stores and by mail order.

2 Spread out the sesame seeds in a heavy frying pan. Toast them over a moderate heat, shaking the pan lightly so that they turn golden all over. Do not let them burn, or the sauce will taste bitter. Set aside 45ml/3 tbsp of the toasted seeds for the garnish and tip the rest into a bowl. Toast the blanched almonds and skinned peanuts in the same way and add them to the bowl with the sesame seeds.

3 Heat half the lard or oil in a frying pan, sauté the chopped onion and garlic for 2–3 minutes, then add the chillies and tomatoes. Cook gently for 10 minutes.

4 Peel the plantain and slice it into short diagonal slices. Add it to the onion mixture with the raisins, prunes, dried oregano, spices and cocoa. Stir in the 250ml/8fl oz/1 cup of the reserved water in which the chillies were soaked. Bring to the boil, stirring, then add the toasted sesame seeds, almonds and peanuts. Cook gently for 10 minutes, stirring frequently; do not let the sauce stick to the pan and burn. Remove from the heat and leave to cool slightly.

5 Blend the sauce in batches in a food processor or blender until smooth. The sauce should be fairly thick, but a little water can be added if you think it is necessary.

6 Heat the remaining lard or oil in a flameproof casserole. Add the turkey and brown over a medium heat.

7 Pour the sauce over the steaks and cover the casserole with foil and a tight-fitting lid. Simmer over a gentle heat for 20–25 minutes or until the turkey is cooked, and the sauce has thickened. Sprinkle with the reserved sesame seeds and the chopped fresh oregano. Turkey *Mole* is traditionally served with a rice dish and warm tortillas.

PORK CASSEROLE WITH CHILLIES AND DRIED FRUIT

USING A TECHNIQUE TAKEN FROM SOUTH AMERICAN COOKING, THIS CASSEROLE IS BASED ON A RICH PASTE OF CHILLIES, SHALLOTS AND NUTS. SERVE IT WITH PLAIN BOILED RICE.

SERVES SIX

INGREDIENTS

25ml/5 tsp plain (all-purpose) flour
1kg/2¼lb shoulder or leg of pork, cut into 5cm/2in cubes
45–60ml/3–4 tbsp olive oil
2 large onions, chopped
2 garlic cloves, finely chopped
600ml/1 pint/2½ cups fruity white wine
105ml/7 tbsp water
115g/4oz/⅔ cup ready-to-eat prunes
115g/4oz/⅔ cup ready-to-eat dried apricots
grated (shredded) rind and juice of 1 small orange
pinch of soft light brown sugar (optional)
30ml/2 tbsp chopped fresh parsley
½–1 fresh red chilli, seeded and finely chopped
salt and ground black pepper
For the paste
3 ancho chillies
2 pasilla chillies
30ml/2 tbsp olive oil
2 shallots, chopped
2 garlic cloves, chopped
1 fresh green chilli, seeded and chopped
10ml/2 tsp ground coriander
5ml/1 tsp mild Spanish paprika or *pimentón dulce*
50g/2oz/½ cup blanched almonds, toasted
15ml/1 tbsp chopped fresh oregano or 7.5ml/1½ tsp dried oregano
plain boiled rice, to serve

1 Make the paste first. Toast the dried chillies in a dry frying pan over a low heat for 1–2 minutes, until they are aromatic, then soak them in a bowl of warm water for 20–30 minutes.

2 Drain the chillies, reserving the soaking water, and discard their stalks and seeds. Preheat the oven to 160°C/325°F/Gas 3.

3 Heat the oil in a small frying pan. Add the shallots, garlic, fresh chilli and ground coriander, and fry over a very low heat for 5 minutes.

4 Transfer the mixture to a food processor or blender and add the drained chillies, paprika or *pimentón dulce*, almonds and oregano. Process the mixture, adding 45–60ml/3–4 tbsp of the chilli soaking liquid to make a smooth workable paste.

5 Season the flour generously with salt and black pepper, then use to coat the pork. Heat 45ml/3 tbsp of the olive oil in a large, heavy pan and fry the pork, stirring frequently, until sealed on all sides. Transfer the pork cubes to a flameproof casserole.

6 If necessary, add the remaining oil to the pan. When it is hot, fry the onions and garlic gently for 8–10 minutes.

COOK'S TIP
A Californian Chardonnay would be a suitably fruity wine to use.

7 Add the wine and water to the pan. Bring up to the boil, reduce the heat and cook for 2 minutes. Stir in half the paste, bring back to the boil and bubble for a few seconds before pouring over the pork.

8 Season lightly with salt and pepper, stir to mix, then cover and cook in the oven for 1½ hours. Increase the oven temperature to 180°C/350°F/Gas 4.

9 Add the prunes, apricots and orange juice to the casserole. Taste the sauce and add more salt and pepper if needed and a pinch of brown sugar if the orange juice has made the sauce a bit tart. Stir, cover, return to the oven and cook for a further 30–45 minutes.

10 Place the casserole over a direct heat and stir in the remaining paste. Simmer, stirring once or twice, for 5 minutes. Sprinkle with the orange rind, chopped parsley and fresh chilli. Serve with boiled rice.

CHILLI RIBS

CHOOSE REALLY MEATY RIBS FOR THIS DISH AND TRIM OFF ANY EXCESS FAT BEFORE COOKING, AS THE JUICES ARE TURNED INTO A DELICIOUS SAUCE. SERVE ON A BED OF SAUERKRAUT WITH CRUSTY BREAD.

2 Heat the oil in a large pan and cook the ribs, turning until well browned. Put in a roasting pan, adding the onion.

3 Mix the braising liquid ingredients and pour over the ribs. Cover with foil then roast for 1½ hours, or until tender. Remove the foil for the last 30 minutes.

SERVES SIX

INGREDIENTS
 25g/1oz/¼ cup plain
  (all-purpose) flour
 5ml/1 tsp salt
 5ml/1 tsp ground black pepper
 1.6kg/3½lb pork spare ribs, cut into
  individual pieces
 30ml/2 tbsp sunflower oil
 1 onion, finely chopped
 15ml/1 tbsp cornflour (cornstarch)
 flat leaf parsley, to garnish
 sauerkraut, to serve
For the braising liquid
 1 garlic clove, crushed
 1 fresh red chilli, seeded and chopped
 45ml/3 tbsp tomato purée (paste)
 30ml/2 tbsp chilli sauce
 30ml/2 tbsp red wine vinegar
 pinch of ground cloves
 600ml/1 pint/2½ cups beef stock

1 Preheat the oven to 180°C/350°F/ Gas 4. Combine the flour, salt and black pepper in a shallow dish. Add the ribs and toss until evenly coated.

COOK'S TIP
Use mild or hot chilli sauce for this dish. If you can track some down, try using 45–60ml/3–4 tbsp ancho chilli and morello cherry glaze instead of the tomato purée and chilli sauce.

4 Tip the juices from the roasting pan into a small pan. Mix the cornflour with a little cold water in a cup, then stir the mixture into the sauce. Bring to the boil, stirring, then simmer for 2–3 minutes until thickened.

5 Serve the ribs on the sauerkraut, with a little sauce. Garnish with parsley. Serve the remaining sauce separately.

SPAGHETTI WITH MEATBALLS

FOR A GREAT INTRODUCTION TO THE CHARM OF CHILLIES, THIS SIMPLE PASTA DISH IS HARD TO BEAT. CHILDREN LOVE THE GENTLE HEAT OF THE SWEET AND SPICY TOMATO SAUCE.

SERVES SIX TO EIGHT

INGREDIENTS
    350g/12oz minced (ground) beef
    1 egg
    60ml/4 tbsp roughly chopped fresh
      flat leaf parsley
    2.5ml/½ tsp crushed dried
      red chillies
    1 thick slice white bread,
      crusts removed
    30ml/2 tbsp milk
    about 30ml/2 tbsp olive oil
    300ml/½ pint/1¼ cups passata
      (bottled strained tomatoes)
    400ml/14fl oz/1⅔ cups
      vegetable stock
    5ml/1 tsp granulated sugar
    350–450g/12oz–1lb fresh or
      dried spaghetti
    salt and ground black pepper
    shavings of Parmesan cheese,
      to serve

1 Put the beef in a large bowl. Add the egg, with half the parsley and half the crushed chillies. Season with plenty of salt and pepper.

2 Tear the bread into small pieces and place these in a small bowl. Moisten with the milk. Leave to soak for a few minutes, then squeeze out the excess milk and crumble the bread over the meat mixture. Mix everything together with a wooden spoon, then use your hands to squeeze and knead the mixture so that it becomes smooth and quite sticky.

3 Wash your hands, rinse them under the cold tap, then pick up small pieces of the mixture and roll them between your palms to make about 40–60 small balls. Place the meatballs on a tray and chill for 30 minutes.

4 Heat the oil in a large non-stick frying pan. Cook the meatballs in batches until browned on all sides. Pour the passata and stock into a large pan. Heat gently, then add the remaining chillies and the sugar, and season. Add the meatballs and bring to the boil. Reduce the heat, and simmer for 20 minutes.

5 Bring a large pan of lightly salted water to the boil and cook the pasta until it is just tender, following the instructions on the packet. Drain and tip it into a large heated bowl. Pour over the sauce and toss gently. Sprinkle with the remaining parsley and shavings of Parmesan cheese. Serve immediately.

FIRE FRY

HERE'S ONE FOR LOVERS OF HOT, SPICY FOOD. TENDER STRIPS OF LAMB, MARINATED IN SPICES AND STIR-FRIED WITH A TOP-DRESSING OF CHILLIES, REALLY HITS THE HOT SPOT.

SERVES FOUR

INGREDIENTS
  225g/8oz lean lamb fillet (tenderloin)
  120ml/4fl oz/½ cup natural
    (plain) yogurt
  1.5ml/¼ tsp ground cardamom
  5ml/1 tsp grated (shredded) fresh
    root ginger
  5ml/1 tsp crushed garlic
  5ml/1 tsp hot chilli powder
  5ml/1 tsp garam masala
  5ml/1 tsp salt
  15ml/1 tbsp corn oil
  2 onions, chopped
  1 bay leaf
  300ml/½ pint/1¼ cups water
  2 fresh red chillies, seeded and
    sliced in strips
  2 fresh green chillies, seeded and
    sliced in strips
  30ml/2 tbsp fresh coriander
    (cilantro) leaves

1 Using a sharp knife, cut the lamb into 7.5–10cm/3–4in pieces, then into strips.

2 In a bowl, whisk the yogurt with the cardamom, ginger, garlic, chilli powder, garam masala and salt. Add the lamb strips and stir to coat them in the mixture. Cover and marinate in a cool place for about 1 hour.

COOK'S TIP
This is a useful recipe for a family divided into those who love chillies and those who don't. Serve the doubters before adding the chillies, or perhaps top their portions with strips of a sweet mild chilli or even a peeled red or green (bell) pepper.

3 Heat the oil in a wok or frying pan and fry the onions for 3–5 minutes, or until they are tender and golden brown.

4 Add the bay leaf and then add the marinated lamb with the yogurt and spices, and toss over a medium heat for about 2–3 minutes.

5 Pour over the water, stir well, then cover and cook for 15–20 minutes over a low heat, stirring occasionally. Once the water has evaporated, stir-fry the mixture for 1 minute.

6 Strew the red and green chillies over the stir-fry, with the fresh coriander. Serve hot. Offer a cooling yogurt dip, if you like.

THAI GREEN BEEF CURRY

CHILLIES ARE THE MAIN INGREDIENT IN GREEN CURRY PASTE, WHICH IS USED FOR THIS FRAGRANT DISH. ALSO INCLUDED ARE THAI AUBERGINES.

SERVES FOUR TO SIX

INGREDIENTS
   15ml/1 tbsp vegetable oil
   45ml/3 tbsp green curry paste
   600ml/1 pint/2½ cups coconut milk
   450g/1lb beef sirloin, cut into long,
     thin slices
   4 kaffir lime leaves, torn
   15–30ml/1–2 tbsp Thai fish sauce
     (*nam pla*)
   5ml/1 tsp palm sugar or soft light
     brown sugar
   150g/5oz small Thai aubergines
     (eggplant), halved
   a small handful of holy basil
   2 fresh green chillies, to garnish

1 Heat the oil in a large pan or wok. Add the green curry paste and fry until fragrant.

2 Stir in half the coconut milk, a little at a time. Cook for about 5–6 minutes, until the milk separates and an oily sheen appears.

VARIATION
You can substitute thinly sliced chicken breast portions for the beef.

3 Add the beef to the pan with the kaffir lime leaves, Thai fish sauce, palm sugar and aubergines. Cook for 2–3 minutes, then stir in the remaining coconut milk.

4 Bring back to a simmer and cook until the meat and aubergines are tender. Stir in the basil just before serving. Finely shred the green chillies and use to garnish the curry.

COOK'S TIP
Thai aubergines look very like unripe tomatoes. Their virtue is that they will cook quickly in a recipe of this kind. They have a delicate flavour and are not so fleshy as the more common large purple-skinned variety. These small aubergines do not need peeling or salting. You may also find small yellow and purple ones.

BEEF WITH PEPPERS AND BLACK BEAN SAUCE

A SPICY, RICH DISH WITH THE DISTINCTIVE TASTE OF BLACK BEAN SAUCE. THIS IS A RECIPE THAT WILL QUICKLY BECOME A FAVOURITE BECAUSE IT IS SO EASY TO PREPARE AND QUICK TO COOK.

SERVES FOUR

INGREDIENTS

    350g/12oz rump (round) steak,
      trimmed and thinly sliced
    20ml/4 tsp vegetable oil
    300ml/½ pint/1¼ cups beef stock
    2 garlic cloves, finely chopped
    5ml/1 tsp grated (shredded) fresh
      root ginger
    1 fresh red chilli, seeded and
      finely chopped
    15ml/1 tbsp black bean sauce
    1 green (bell) pepper, seeded and
      cut into 2.5cm/1in squares
    15ml/1 tbsp dry sherry
    5ml/1 tsp cornflour (cornstarch)
    5ml/1 tsp granulated sugar
    45ml/3 tbsp cold water
    salt
    cooked rice noodles, to serve

1 Place the rump steak in a bowl. Add 5ml/1 tsp of the oil and stir to coat.

VARIATIONS

• Use any chilli you like. Habanero, with its hint of apricot flavour, would be a good if very hot choice.
• For extra colour, use a red or orange (bell) pepper or even a yellow Hungarian wax chilli.

2 Bring the stock to the boil in a pan. Add the beef and cook for 2 minutes, stirring constantly to prevent the slices from sticking together. Drain the beef and set aside. Retain the stock for use in another recipe.

3 Heat the remaining oil in a wok. Stir-fry the garlic, ginger and chilli with the black bean sauce for a few seconds. Add the pepper squares and a little water. Cook for about 2 minutes more, then stir in the sherry. Add the beef slices to the pan, spoon the sauce over and reheat.

4 Mix the cornflour and sugar to a cream with the water. Pour the mixture into the pan. Cook, stirring, until the sauce has thickened. Season with salt. Serve immediately, with rice noodles.

COOK'S TIP

To make beef stock, brown 1kg/2¼lb beef or veal bones in an oven heated to 180°C/350°F/Gas 4 for 30 minutes. Put the bones in a pan with a bay leaf and some peppercorns. Cover with water. Add the washed skins of 2 onions, 2 chopped carrot and 1 celery stick. Bring to the boil, simmer for 40 minutes. Strain.

BEEF ENCHILADAS WITH RED SAUCE

DRIED CHILLIES ARE WONDERFUL PANTRY STAPLES. IT IS WORTH HAVING A SUPPLY OF SEVERAL DIFFERENT TYPES, SO YOU'LL ALWAYS HAVE THE MEANS TO MAKE SPICY DISHES LIKE THIS ONE.

SERVES TWO TO THREE

INGREDIENTS

500g/1¼lb rump (round) steak, cut
  into 5cm/2in cubes
2 ancho chillies, seeded
2 pasilla chillies, seeded
30ml/2 tbsp vegetable oil
2 garlic cloves, crushed
10ml/2 tsp dried oregano
2.5ml/½ tsp ground cumin
7 fresh corn tortillas
shredded onion and fresh flat leaf
  parsley, to garnish
mango and chilli salsa,
  to serve

1 Put the cubed rump steak in a pan and cover with water. Bring to the boil, then lower the heat and simmer for 1–1½ hours, or until very tender.

2 Meanwhile, put the dried chillies in a bowl and pour over hot water to cover. Leave to soak for 20–30 minutes, then tip the contents of the bowl into a blender and whizz to a smooth paste.

3 Drain the steak and let it cool, reserving 250ml/8fl oz/1 cup of the cooking liquid. Meanwhile, heat the oil in a large frying pan and fry the garlic, oregano and cumin for 2 minutes.

4 Stir in the chilli paste and the reserved cooking liquid from the beef. Tear 1 of the tortillas into small pieces and add it to the mixture. Bring to the boil, then lower the heat. Simmer for 10 minutes, stirring occasionally, until the sauce has thickened. Shred the steak, using 2 forks, and stir it into the sauce. Heat through for a few minutes.

5 Spoon some of the meat mixture on to each tortilla and roll it up to make an enchilada. Keep the enchiladas in a warmed dish until you have rolled them all. Garnish the enchiladas with shreds of onion and fresh flat leaf parsley, and serve immediately with mango and chilli salsa.

VARIATIONS
• For a richer version, place the rolled enchiladas side by side in a gratin dish. Pour over 300ml/½ pint/1¼ cups sour cream and 75g/3oz/¾ cup grated (shredded) Cheddar cheese. Grill (broil) for 5 minutes or until the cheese melts and the sauce begins to bubble. Serve immediately, with the salsa.
• For a sharper tasting cheese topping, substitute Parmesan cheese for half the quantity of Cheddar.

MADRAS CURRY <u>WITH</u> SPICY RICE

CHILLIES ARE AN INDISPENSABLE INGREDIENT OF A HOT MADRAS CURRY. AFTER LONG, GENTLE SIMMERING, THEY MERGE WITH THE OTHER FLAVOURINGS TO GIVE A DELECTABLE RESULT.

SERVES FOUR

INGREDIENTS

   30ml/2 tbsp vegetable oil
   25g/1oz/2 tbsp ghee or butter
   675g/1½lb stewing beef, cut into
     bitesize cubes
   1 onion, chopped
   3 green cardamom pods
   2 fresh green chillies, seeded and
     finely chopped
   2.5cm/1in piece of fresh root
     ginger, grated (shredded)
   2 garlic cloves, crushed
   15ml/1 tbsp Madras curry paste
   5ml/1 tsp ground cumin
   5ml/1 tsp ground coriander
   150ml/¼ pint/⅔ cup beef stock
   salt
For the rice
   225g/8oz/generous 1 cup
     basmati rice
   15ml/1 tbsp sunflower oil
   25g/1oz/2 tbsp ghee or butter
   1 onion, finely chopped
   1 garlic clove, crushed
   5ml/1 tsp ground cumin
   2.5ml/½ tsp ground coriander
   4 green cardamom pods
   1 cinnamon stick
   1 small red (bell) pepper, seeded
     and diced
   1 small green (bell) pepper, seeded
     and diced
   300ml/½ pint/1¼ cups chicken stock

1 Heat half the oil with half the ghee or butter in a large, shallow pan. Fry the meat, in batches if necessary, until browned on all sides. Transfer to a plate and set aside.

2 Heat the remaining oil and ghee or butter and fry the onion for about 3–4 minutes until softened. Add the cardamom pods and fry for 1 minute, then stir in the chillies, ginger and garlic, and fry for 2 minutes more.

3 Stir in the curry paste, ground cumin and coriander, then return the meat to the pan. Stir in the stock. Season with salt, bring to the boil, then reduce the heat and simmer very gently for 1–1½ hours, until the meat is tender.

4 When the curry is almost ready, prepare the rice. Put it in a bowl and pour over boiling water to cover. Set aside for 10 minutes, then drain, rinse under cold water and drain again. The rice will still be uncooked but should have lost its brittleness.

VARIATION
If you like, you can serve plain boiled rice with this curry. Put the rice in a sieve and rinse it under cold water. Place in a pan with 5ml/1 tsp salt, and add water to come 5cm/2in above the level of the rice. Bring to the boil and simmer for 9–12 minutes. Drain and serve.

5 Heat the oil and ghee or butter in a flameproof casserole and fry the onion and garlic gently for 3–4 minutes until softened and lightly browned.

6 Stir in the ground cumin and coriander, green cardamom pods and cinnamon stick. Fry for 1 minute, then add the diced peppers.

7 Add the rice, stirring to coat the grains in the spice mixture, and pour in the chicken stock. Bring to the boil, then reduce the heat, cover the pan tightly and simmer for about 8–10 minutes, or until the rice is tender and the stock has been absorbed. Spoon into a bowl and serve with the curry.

COOK'S TIPS
• The curry should be fairly dry, but take care that it does not catch on the base of the pan. If you want to leave it unattended, cook it in a heavy pan. Alternatively, cook it in a flameproof casserole, in an oven preheated to 180°C/350°F/Gas 4.
• Offer a little mango chutney, if you like, and if you want to cool the heat, a bowl of yogurt raita.

SHREDDED BEEF WITH CHILLIES

THE ESSENCE OF THIS RECIPE IS THAT THE BEEF IS CUT INTO VERY FINE STRIPS. THIS IS EASIER TO ACHIEVE IF THE MEAT IS PLACED IN THE FREEZER FOR 30 MINUTES BEFORE BEING SLICED.

3 Heat a wok and add half the oil. When it is hot, stir-fry the onion and ginger for 3–4 minutes, then lift out with a slotted spoon and set aside. Add the carrot, stir-fry for 3–4 minutes until slightly softened, then transfer to a plate and keep warm.

4 Heat the remaining oil in the wok, then quickly add the beef, with the marinade, followed by the chillies. Cook over high heat for 2 minutes, stirring all the time.

SERVES TWO

INGREDIENTS
 225g/8oz rump (round) or fillet
 (tenderloin) of beef
 15ml/1 tbsp each light and dark
 soy sauce
 15ml/1 tbsp rice wine or
 medium-dry sherry
 5ml/1 tsp dark brown soft sugar
 90ml/6 tbsp vegetable oil
 1 large onion, thinly sliced
 2.5cm/1in piece fresh root ginger,
 peeled and grated (shredded)
 1–2 carrots, cut into matchsticks
 2–3 fresh chillies, halved, seeded
 (optional) and chopped
salt and ground black pepper
fresh chives, to garnish

1 With a sharp knife, slice the beef very thinly, then cut each slice into fine strips or shreds.

2 In a bowl, mix the light and dark soy sauces with the rice wine or sherry and sugar. Add the strips of beef and stir well to ensure that they are evenly coated with the marinade. Cover and marinate in a cool place for 30 minutes.

5 Return the fried onion and ginger to the wok and stir-fry for 1 minute more. Season with salt and pepper to taste, cover and cook for 30 seconds. Spoon the meat into 2 warmed bowls and add the carrot strips. Garnish with fresh chives and serve.

COOK'S TIPS
• Use dried chillies if you prefer. Snap them in half, shake out the seeds, then soak them in hot water for 20–30 minutes.
• If you enjoy your food really fiery, don't bother to remove the seeds from the chillies.

CHILLI CON CARNE

*THIS FAMOUS TEX-MEX STEW HAS BECOME AN INTERNATIONAL FAVOURITE. SERVE IT WITH RICE OR
BAKED POTATOES AND A HEARTY GREEN SALAD.*

SERVES EIGHT

INGREDIENTS

   1.2kg/2½lb lean braising steak
   30ml/2 tbsp sunflower oil
   1 large onion, chopped
   2 garlic cloves, finely chopped
   15ml/1 tbsp plain (all-purpose) flour
   300ml/½ pint/1¼ cups red wine
   300ml/½ pint/1¼ cups beef stock
   30ml/2 tbsp tomato purée (paste)
   salt and ground black pepper
For the beans
   30ml/2 tbsp olive oil
   1 onion, chopped
   1 fresh red chilli, seeded
    and chopped
   2 × 400g/14oz cans red kidney
    beans, drained and rinsed
   400g/14oz can chopped tomatoes
For the topping
   6 tomatoes, peeled and chopped
   1 fresh green chilli, seeded
    and chopped
   30ml/2 tbsp chopped fresh chives
   30ml/2 tbsp chopped fresh coriander
    (cilantro), plus sprigs to garnish
   150ml/¼ pint/⅔ cup sour cream

1 Cut the meat into thick strips, then
cut it crossways into small cubes. Heat
the oil in a large, flameproof casserole.
Add the chopped onion and garlic, and
cook until softened but not coloured.
Season the flour and place it on a plate,
then toss a batch of meat in it.

VARIATION
This stew is also delicious served with
tortillas. Wrap the tortillas in foil and
warm through in the oven.

2 Use a slotted spoon to remove the
onion from the pan, then add the
floured beef and cook over a high heat
until browned on all sides. Remove from
the pan and set aside, then flour and
brown another batch of meat.

3 When the last batch of meat has been
browned, return the reserved meat and
the onion to the pan. Stir in the wine,
stock and tomato purée. Bring to the
boil, reduce the heat and simmer for
45 minutes, or until the beef is tender.

4 Meanwhile, for the beans, heat the
olive oil in a frying pan and cook the
onion and chilli until softened. Stir in
the kidney beans and tomatoes, and
simmer gently for 20–25 minutes, or
until thickened and reduced.

5 Mix the tomatoes, chilli, chives and
coriander for the topping. Ladle the
meat mixture on to warmed plates. Add
a layer of bean mixture and tomato
topping. Finish with sour cream and
garnish with coriander leaves.

If you've ever damned vegetarian food as dull, these recipes will fire you with enthusiasm. Go for the burn with exciting and unusual dishes such as Black Bean and Chilli Burritos or Sweet Rice with Hot Sour Chickpeas. For spice with more substance, try Okra, Chilli and Tomato Tagine, Chilli Beans with Lemon and Ginger or Sichuan Sizzler.

Vegetarian Meals and Side Dishes

PEPPERS FILLED WITH SPICED VEGETABLES

JALAPEÑO CHILLIES AND INDIAN SPICES SEASON THE VEGETABLE STUFFING IN THESE COLOURFUL BAKED PEPPERS. SERVE THESE WITH PLAIN RICE, CUCUMBER SLICES AND A LENTIL DHAL.

SERVES SIX

INGREDIENTS

   6 large evenly shaped red or yellow
     (bell) peppers
   500g/1¼lb potatoes, peeled, halved
     if large
   1–2 jalapeños or other fresh green
     chillies, seeded and chopped
   1 small onion, chopped
   4–5 garlic cloves, chopped
   5cm/2in piece of fresh root
     ginger, chopped
   105ml/7 tbsp water
   90–105ml/6–7 tbsp groundnut
     (peanut) oil
   1 aubergine (eggplant), cut into
     1cm/½in dice
   10ml/2 tsp cumin seeds
   5ml/1 tsp kalonji seeds
   2.5ml/½ tsp ground turmeric
   5ml/1 tsp ground coriander
   5ml/1 tsp ground toasted
     cumin seeds
   1–2 pinches of cayenne pepper
   about 30ml/2 tbsp lemon juice
   salt and ground black pepper
   30ml/2 tbsp chopped fresh coriander
     (cilantro), to garnish

1 Cut the tops off the peppers and pull out the central core from each, keeping the shells intact. Shake out any remaining seeds. Cut a thin slice off the base of the peppers, if necessary, to make them stand upright.

2 Bring a large pan of lightly salted water to the boil. Add the peppers and cook for 5–6 minutes. Lift out and drain them upside down in a colander.

3 Bring the water in the pan back to the boil, add the potatoes and cook for 10–12 minutes, until just tender. Drain thoroughly, put on one side to cool, then cut into 1cm/½in dice.

4 Put the green chillies, onion, garlic and ginger in a food processor or blender with 60ml/4 tbsp of the water and process to a purée. Preheat the oven to 190°C/375°F/Gas 5.

5 Heat 45ml/3 tbsp of the oil in a large, deep frying pan and cook the aubergine, stirring occasionally, until browned on all sides. Remove from the pan and set aside. Add another 30ml/2 tbsp of the oil to the pan and sauté the potatoes until lightly browned. Remove from the pan and set aside.

6 If necessary, add another 15ml/1 tbsp oil to the pan, then add the cumin and kalonji seeds. Fry briefly until the seeds darken, then add the turmeric, coriander and ground cumin. Cook for 15 seconds. Stir in the chilli purée and fry, scraping the pan with a spatula, until the mixture begins to brown. Do not let it burn.

7 Return the potatoes and aubergines to the pan, and season with salt, pepper and 1–2 pinches of cayenne. Pour in the remaining measured water and 15ml/1 tbsp lemon juice. Cook, stirring, until the liquid evaporates.

8 Place the peppers on a baking tray and fill with the potato mixture. Brush the pepper skins with a little oil and bake for 30–35 minutes, until cooked. Allow to cool a little, then sprinkle with a little more lemon juice, garnish with the coriander and serve.

COOK'S TIPS
• Try using poblano chillies instead of the sweet peppers.
• The spice kalonji, also known as nigella, is a very tiny black seed that closely resembles the onion seed. It is available from most supermarkets and Indian foodstores.

VARIATIONS
• Instead of serving with rice and a lentil dhal, try Indian breads and a cucumber or mint yogurt raita.
• Substitute carrots and parsnips for the potatoes.

CUCUMBER AND ALFALFA TORTILLAS

SERVED WITH A PIQUANT CHILLI SALSA, THESE FILLED TORTILLAS ARE EXTREMELY EASY TO PREPARE AT HOME AND MAKE A MARVELLOUS LIGHT LUNCH OR SUPPER DISH.

3 To make the tortillas, place the flour and salt in a food processor or blender, add the oil and blend. Gradually add the water (the amount will vary depending on the flour). Stop adding water when a stiff dough has formed. Turn out on to a floured board and knead for about 5–10 minutes until smooth. Cover with a damp cloth.

4 Divide the mixture into 8 pieces. Knead each piece for a couple of minutes and form into a ball. Flatten and roll out each ball to form a 23cm/ 9in diameter circle.

5 Heat an ungreased heavy frying pan. Cook 1 tortilla at a time for about 30 seconds on each side. Wrap the cooked tortillas in a clean dishtowel. Make the 7 remaining balls of dough into tortillas in the same way.

SERVES FOUR

INGREDIENTS
   225g/8oz/2 cups plain
     (all-purpose) flour
   pinch of salt
   45ml/3 tbsp olive oil
   120–150ml/4–5fl oz/½–⅔ cup
     warm water
   lime wedges, to garnish
For the salsa
   1 red onion, finely chopped
   1 fresh red chilli, seeded and
     finely chopped
   30ml/2 tbsp chopped fresh dill
   ½ cucumber, peeled and chopped
   175g/6oz/3 cups alfalfa sprouts
For the avocado sauce
   1 large avocado, halved, peeled
     and stoned (pitted)
   juice of 1 lime
   25g/1oz/2 tbsp soft goat's cheese
   pinch of paprika

1 Make the salsa. Put the onion and chilli in a bowl. Add the dill, cucumber and alfalfa sprouts, and mix well. Cover.

6 Take the covering off the avocado sauce and dust the top with paprika. To serve, spread each tortilla with a spoonful of avocado sauce, top with salsa and roll up. Garnish with lime wedges. A green salad would be a good accompaniment.

COOK'S TIP
When peeling the avocado, be sure to scrape off the bright green flesh from immediately under the skin as this gives the sauce its vivid colour.

2 To make the sauce, place the avocado, lime juice and goat's cheese in a blender and process. Scrape into a bowl. Cover with clear film (plastic wrap).

BLACK BEAN AND CHILLI BURRITOS

TORTILLAS ARE A WONDERFULLY ADAPTABLE FOOD. HERE THEY ARE FILLED WITH BEANS, CHEESE AND SALSA, AND SPIKED WITH CHILLI. A SHORT PERIOD OF BAKING IN THE OVEN AND THEY'RE READY TO EAT.

SERVES FOUR

INGREDIENTS

225g/8oz/1¼ cups dried black beans, soaked in water overnight
1 bay leaf
45ml/3 tbsp coarse salt
1 small red onion, finely chopped
225g/8oz/2 cups grated (shredded) Cheddar cheese or Monterey Jack
45ml/3 tbsp chopped pickled jalapeño chillies
15ml/1 tbsp chopped fresh coriander (cilantro)
900ml/1½ pints/3¾ cups tomato salsa
8 wheat flour tortillas
salt and ground black pepper
diced avocado, to serve

1 Drain the beans and put them in a large pan. Add fresh cold water to cover and the bay leaf. Bring to the boil, then reduce the heat, cover and simmer for 30 minutes. Add the salt and continue simmering for about 30 minutes more, or until the beans are tender. Drain and tip into a bowl. Discard the bay leaf.

2 Grease a rectangular baking dish. Add the onion, half the cheese, the jalapeños, coriander and 250ml/8fl oz/1 cup of the salsa to the beans. Stir well and add salt and pepper if needed. Preheat the oven to 180°C/350°F/Gas 4.

3 Place 1 tortilla on a board. Spread a large spoonful of the filling down the middle, then roll up to enclose the filling. Place the burrito in the dish, seam side down. Repeat to make 7 more.

4 Sprinkle the remaining cheese over the burritos. Bake for 15 minutes, until all the cheese melts.

5 Serve the burritos immediately, with avocado and the remaining salsa.

PANCAKES STUFFED <u>WITH</u> LIGHTLY SPICED SQUASH

IN ORDER TO APPRECIATE THE INDIVIDUAL FLAVOURS OF THE BUTTERNUT SQUASH, LEEKS AND CHICORY IN THESE PANCAKES, IT IS IMPORTANT NOT TO OVERDO THE CHILLI.

SERVES FOUR

INGREDIENTS
  115g/4oz/1 cup plain (all-purpose) flour
  50g/2oz/generous ⅓ cup yellow
    corn meal
  2.5ml/½ tsp salt
  2.5ml/½ tsp chilli powder
  2 large (US extra large) eggs
  450ml/¾ pint/scant 2 cups milk
  65g/2½oz/5 tbsp butter
  vegetable oil, for greasing
  25g/1oz/⅓ cup freshly grated
    (shredded) Parmesan cheese
For the filling
  30ml/2 tbsp olive oil
  450g/1lb butternut squash (peeled
    weight), seeded
  large pinch of dried red chilli flakes
  2 large leeks, thickly sliced
  2.5ml/½ tsp chopped fresh or
    dried thyme
  3 chicory (Belgian endive) heads,
    thickly sliced
  115g/4oz full-flavoured goat's
    cheese, cut into cubes
  90g/3½oz/scant 1 cup walnuts or
    pecan nuts, roughly chopped
  30ml/2 tbsp chopped fresh flat
    leaf parsley
  salt and ground black pepper

2 When ready to cook the pancakes, melt 25g/1oz/2 tbsp of the butter and stir it into the batter. Heat a lightly greased 18cm/7in heavy frying pan or crêpe pan. Pour about 60ml/4 tbsp of the batter into the pan, tilt it so that the batter forms a pancake and cook for 2–3 minutes, until set and lightly browned underneath. Turn and cook the pancake on the other side for 2–3 minutes. Lightly grease the pan after every second pancake.

3 Make the filling. Heat the oil in a large pan. Add the squash and cook, stirring frequently, for 10 minutes, until almost tender. Add the chilli flakes and cook, stirring, for a further 1–2 minutes. Stir in the leeks and thyme, and cook for 4–5 minutes more.

5 Preheat the oven to 200°C/400°F/ Gas 6. Lightly grease an ovenproof dish. Either layer the pancakes with the filling to make a stack in the dish or stuff each pancake with 30–45ml/2–3 tbsp filling. Roll or fold the pancakes to enclose the filling and place in the dish.

6 Sprinkle the grated Parmesan over the pancakes. Melt the remaining butter and drizzle it over the layered or filled pancakes. Bake for 10–15 minutes, until the cheese is bubbling and the pancakes are piping hot. Serve immediately.

COOK'S TIP
This can all be prepared in advance, but make sure the filling is cold before adding to the pancakes.

VARIATIONS
• Fennel could be used instead of chicory, and pumpkin, other varieties of winter squash or courgette (zucchini) instead of butternut squash.
• If you like, you can add a fresh chilli, but make it a mild one, such as Anaheim. Roast and peel it first.

1 Sift the flour, corn meal, salt and chilli powder into a bowl. Make a well in the centre. Add the eggs and a little of the milk. Whisk the eggs and milk, gradually incorporating the dry ingredients and adding more milk to make a batter with a consistency like that of thick cream.

4 Add the chicory and cook, stirring frequently, for 4–5 minutes, until the leeks are cooked and the chicory is hot, but still with some bite to its texture. Cool slightly, then stir in the cheese, nuts and parsley. Season the mixture well with salt and pepper.

CARIBBEAN RED BEAN CHILLI

WHEN PULSES PARTNER CHILLIES, THE HEAT SEEMS TO BE MODERATED SLIGHTLY, SO THIS LENTIL AND RED KIDNEY BEAN MIXTURE IS A GOOD VEHICLE FOR A HABANERO OR SCOTCH BONNET CHILLI.

3 Add the lentils, thyme, cumin, soy sauce, chilli, mixed spice and vegetarian oyster sauce, if using.

4 Cover and simmer for 40 minutes or until the lentils are cooked, stirring occasionally and adding more water if the lentils begin to dry out.

5 Stir in the red kidney beans and sugar and continue cooking for 10 minutes, adding a little extra stock or water if necessary. Season to taste with salt. Serve the chilli hot with boiled rice and sweetcorn.

VARIATION
You could substitute a can of black beans for the red kidney beans.

SERVES FOUR

INGREDIENTS
  30ml/2 tbsp vegetable oil
  1 onion, chopped
  400g/14oz can chopped tomatoes
  2 garlic cloves, crushed
  300ml/½ pint/1¼ cups white wine
  about 300ml/½ pint/1¼ cups stock
  115g/4oz/½ cup red lentils
  5ml/1 tsp dried thyme
  10ml/2 tsp ground cumin
  45ml/3 tbsp dark soy sauce
  ½–1 habanero or Scotch bonnet
    chilli, seeded and finely chopped
  5ml/1 tsp mixed (pumpkin pie) spice
  15ml/1 tbsp vegetarian oyster
    sauce (optional)
  225g/8oz can red kidney
    beans, drained
  10ml/2 tsp granulated sugar
  salt
  boiled rice and sweetcorn, to serve

1 Heat the oil in a large pan and fry the onion over a medium heat for a few minutes until slightly softened.

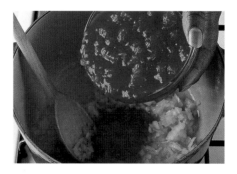

2 Add the tomatoes and garlic, cook for 10 minutes, then stir in the white wine and stock.

COOK'S TIP
It's a good idea to cut any surplus chillies in half, wrap the halves separately, and freeze them.

SWEET RICE WITH HOT SOUR CHICKPEAS

CONTRASTING FLAVOURS CAN BE JUST AS INTERESTING AS COMPLEMENTARY ONES. CHICKPEAS, SPICED WITH CHILLIES AND SOURED WITH LEMON, TASTE REMARKABLY GOOD WITH SWEET RICE.

SERVES SIX

INGREDIENTS

350g/12oz/1⅔ cups dried chickpeas, soaked overnight in water
60ml/4 tbsp vegetable oil
1 large onion, very finely chopped
2 tomatoes, peeled and finely chopped
15ml/1 tbsp ground coriander
15ml/1 tbsp ground cumin
5ml/1 tsp ground fenugreek
5ml/1 tsp ground cinnamon
1–2 fresh hot green chillies, seeded and finely sliced
2.5cm/1in piece of fresh root ginger, grated (shredded)
60ml/4 tbsp lemon juice
15ml/1 tbsp chopped fresh coriander (cilantro)
salt and ground black pepper
For the rice
40g/1½oz/3 tbsp ghee or butter
4 green cardamom pods
4 cloves
650ml/22fl oz/2¾ cups water
350g/12oz/1¾ cups basmati rice (see Cook's Tip)
5–10ml/1–2 tsp granulated sugar
5–6 saffron threads, soaked in warm water

1 Drain the chickpeas well and place them in a large pan. Pour in water to cover, bring to the boil, then lower the heat, cover and simmer for 1–1¼ hours until tender. Drain, reserving the cooking liquid.

COOK'S TIP
Soak the rice in 1.2 litres/2 pints/5 cups water for 30 minutes. Drain.

2 Heat the oil in a pan. Reserve about 30ml/2 tbsp of the chopped onion and add the remainder to the pan. Fry over a medium heat for 4–5 minutes, stirring. Add the tomatoes. Cook over a low to medium heat for 5–6 minutes.

3 Stir in the ground coriander, cumin, fenugreek and cinnamon. Cook for 30 seconds, then add the chickpeas and 350ml/12fl oz/1½ cups of the reserved cooking liquid. Season with salt, then cover and simmer very gently for 15–20 minutes, stirring occasionally and adding more liquid if necessary.

4 For the rice, melt the ghee or butter in a pan and fry the cardamom and cloves for a few minutes. Pour in the water, then add the rice. Bring to the boil, reduce the heat to very low and cover tightly. Cook for 15 minutes or until the liquid has been absorbed. Stir the sugar and saffron liquid into the rice. Replace the lid.

5 Mix the reserved onion with the sliced chilli(es), ginger and lemon juice, and stir the mixture into the chickpeas. Add the chopped coriander, adjust the seasoning and serve with the rice.

OKRA, CHILLI AND TOMATO TAGINE

THE WORD "TAGINE" USUALLY CONJURES UP AN IMAGE OF A SPICY LAMB AND APRICOT STEW, BUT THIS VEGETARIAN VERSION IS EQUALLY AUTHENTIC.

SERVES FOUR

INGREDIENTS

350g/12oz okra
5–6 tomatoes
2 small onions
2 garlic cloves, crushed
1 fresh green chilli, seeded
5ml/1 tsp paprika
small handful of fresh
  coriander (cilantro)
175ml/6fl oz/¾ cup water
30ml/2 tbsp sunflower oil
juice of 1 lemon

1 Trim the okra and then cut into 1cm/½in lengths. Peel and seed the tomatoes and chop roughly.

2 Roughly chop 1 of the onions and place in a food processor or blender with the garlic, chilli, paprika, coriander and 60ml/4 tbsp of the water. Blend to a paste.

COOK'S TIP
A tagine is an earthenware dish with a tall conical lid, which has given its name to slowly simmered stews. It is used in North African cooking.

3 Heat the sunflower oil in a large pan. Thinly slice the second onion in rings and fry in the oil for 5–6 minutes until golden brown. Using a slotted spoon, transfer the fried onion rings to a plate lined with crumpled kitchen paper. Set aside.

4 Reduce the heat and scrape the onion and coriander mixture into the pan. Cook for 1–2 minutes, stirring frequently, and then add the okra, tomatoes, lemon juice and remaining water. Stir well to mix, cover tightly and simmer over a low heat for about 15 minutes until the okra is tender.

5 Transfer the tagine to a warmed serving dish, sprinkle with the fried onion rings and serve immediately while hot.

VARIATION
To make this more substantial, add extra vegetables, such as aubergine (eggplant), carrots and leeks.

CHILLI BEANS WITH BASMATI RICE

RED KIDNEY BEANS, TOMATOES AND CHILLI MAKE A GREAT COMBINATION. SERVE WITH PASTA OR PITTA BREAD INSTEAD OF RICE, IF YOU PREFER.

SERVES FOUR

INGREDIENTS
  350g/12oz/1¾ cups basmati rice
  30ml/2 tbsp olive oil
  1 large onion, chopped
  1 garlic clove, crushed
  15ml/1 tbsp hot chilli powder
  15ml/1 tbsp plain (all-purpose) flour
  15ml/1 tbsp tomato purée (paste)
  400g/14oz can chopped tomatoes
  400g/14oz can red kidney beans,
    rinsed and drained
  150ml/¼ pint/⅔ cup hot
    vegetable stock
  salt and ground black pepper
  chopped fresh parsley, to garnish

3 Stir in the tomato purée, chopped tomatoes and kidney beans with the hot vegetable stock. Cover and cook for 12 minutes, stirring occasionally to prevent the beans from sticking.

4 Season the mixture with salt and pepper. Drain the rice and divide among serving plates. Ladle the chilli beans on to the plates, garnish with a sprinkling of chopped fresh parsley and serve.

1 Wash the rice several times under cold running water. Drain well. Bring a large pan of water to the boil. Add the rice and cook for 10–12 minutes, until tender. Meanwhile, heat the oil in a frying pan. Add the onion and garlic and cook for 2 minutes.

2 Stir the chilli powder and flour into the onion and garlic mixture. Cook gently for 2 minutes, stirring frequently to prevent the onions from browning.

BENGALI-STYLE VEGETABLES

THIS HOT DRY CURRY USES SPICES THAT DO NOT REQUIRE LONG SLOW COOKING. YOU CAN PREPARE AND PARTIALLY COOK THE VEGETABLES IN ADVANCE AND COMPLETE THE DISH QUICKLY LATER IN THE DAY.

SERVES FOUR

INGREDIENTS

½ cauliflower, broken into florets
1 large potato, peeled and cut into
  2.5cm/1in dice
115g/4oz green beans, trimmed
2 courgettes (zucchini), halved
  lengthways and sliced
2 fresh green chillies
2.5cm/1in piece of fresh root
  ginger, peeled
120ml/4fl oz/½ cup natural
  (plain) yogurt
10ml/2 tsp ground coriander
2.5ml/½ tsp ground turmeric
25g/1oz/2 tbsp ghee
2.5ml/½ tsp garam masala
5ml/1 tsp cumin seeds
10ml/2 tsp granulated sugar
pinch each of ground cloves, ground
  cinnamon and ground cardamom
salt and ground black pepper

1 Bring a large pan of water to the boil. Add the cauliflower florets and diced potato, and cook for 5 minutes. Add the beans and courgettes, and cook for 2–3 minutes.

2 Meanwhile, cut the chillies in half, then scrape out and discard the seeds using a very sharp knife. Roughly chop the flesh. Finely chop the ginger. Mix the chillies and ginger together in a small bowl.

3 Drain the vegetables and tip them into a bowl. Add the chilli and ginger mixture, with the yogurt, ground coriander and turmeric. Season with plenty of salt and pepper, and mix well.

4 Heat the ghee in a large frying pan. Add the vegetable mixture and cook over a high heat for 2 minutes, stirring from time to time.

5 Stir in the garam masala and cumin seeds, and cook for 2 minutes. Stir in the sugar, ground cloves, cinnamon and cardamom, and cook for 1 minute or until all the liquid has evaporated. Serve at once.

COOK'S TIPS
• Ghee has a burning point higher than the best oils, so it is very good for frying and searing.
• An alternative to ghee is to add a little groundnut (peanut) oil to ordinary butter. It allows the frying temperature to be reached without burning.

CHILLI BEANS WITH LEMON AND GINGER

AN EXTREMELY QUICK AND DELICIOUS MEAL, MADE WITH CANNED BEANS FOR SPEED. YOU CAN USE ANY RED CHILLI, SUCH AS FRESH CAYENNES OR RED FRESNO, OR REHYDRATE A DRIED PASILLA OR TWO.

SERVES FOUR

INGREDIENTS
   5cm/2in piece fresh ginger root,
      peeled and roughly chopped
   3 garlic cloves, roughly chopped
   250ml/8fl oz/1 cup cold water
   15ml/1 tbsp sunflower oil
   1 large onion, thinly sliced
   1 fresh red chilli, seeded and
      finely chopped
   1.5ml/¼ tsp cayenne pepper
   10ml/2 tsp ground cumin
   5ml/1 tsp ground coriander
   2.5ml/½ tsp ground turmeric
   30ml/2 tbsp lemon juice
   75g/3oz/1½ cups chopped fresh
      coriander (cilantro)
   400g/14oz can black-eyed beans,
      (peas) drained and rinsed
   400g/14oz can aduki beans, drained
      and rinsed
   400g/14oz can haricot (navy) beans,
      drained and rinsed
   ground black pepper

1 Place the ginger, garlic and 60ml/ 4 tbsp of the cold water in a blender or food processor and whizz until smooth.

2 Heat the oil in a pan. Add the onion and chilli, and cook gently for 5 minutes until softened.

3 Add the cayenne, cumin, coriander and turmeric, and stir-fry for 1 minute.

VARIATION
Substitute chickpeas or butter (lima) beans for the haricot beans.

4 Stir in the ginger and garlic paste from the blender or food processor and cook for another minute.

5 Pour in the remaining water, then add the lemon juice and fresh coriander, stir well and bring to the boil. Cover the pan tightly and cook gently over a low heat for 5 minutes.

6 Stir in all the beans and cook for a further 5–10 minutes, until piping hot. Season with pepper and serve.

COOK'S TIPS
• If time allows, make this the day before you intend to serve it, so that the flavours have time to blend and become absorbed by the beans.
• Chillies in a dish such as this one sometimes have a mellower taste after standing, so what may have seemed explosive at the onset may become less so. You can't count on this result, however!
• Don't add extra salt to the beans: canned ones tend to be ready-salted.
• Cooked in this way, these beans are very good served cold in a three-bean salad.
• Add any leftovers to soup.

SICHUAN SIZZLER

THIS DISH IS ALSO KNOWN AS FISH-FRAGRANT AUBERGINE, AS THE FLAVOURINGS OFTEN ACCOMPANY FISH. IF YOU USE TINY AUBERGINES, OMIT THE SALTING PROCESS, HALVE AND DEEP-FRY THEM.

SERVES FOUR

INGREDIENTS

2 medium aubergines (eggplant)
5ml/1 tsp salt
3 dried red chillies
groundnut (peanut) oil, for
  deep-frying
3–4 garlic cloves, finely chopped
1cm/½in piece fresh root ginger,
  finely chopped
4 spring onions (scallions), cut into
  2.5cm/1in lengths (white and green
  parts kept separate)
15ml/1 tbsp Chinese rice wine or
  medium-dry sherry
15ml/1 tbsp light soy sauce
5ml/1 tsp granulated sugar
1.5ml/¼ tsp ground roasted
  Sichuan peppercorns
15ml/1 tbsp Chinese rice vinegar
5ml/1 tsp sesame oil

1 Trim the aubergines and cut them into strips, about 4cm/1½in wide and 7.5cm/3in long. Place the aubergines in a colander and sprinkle over the salt. Leave for 30 minutes, then rinse them thoroughly under cold running water. Pat dry with kitchen paper.

2 Meanwhile, soak the chillies in a bowl of warm water for 20–30 minutes. Then drain and pat dry with kitchen paper.

3 Cut each chilli into 3–4 pieces, discarding the seeds.

4 Half-fill a wok with oil and heat to 180°C/350°F. Deep-fry the aubergine pieces until golden brown. Drain on kitchen paper. Pour off most of the oil from the wok.

5 Reheat the oil left in the wok and add the garlic, ginger, chillies and the white spring onion. Stir-fry for 30 seconds.

6 Add the aubergine and toss over the heat for 1–2 minutes. Stir in the rice wine or sherry, soy sauce, sugar, ground peppercorns and rice vinegar. Stir-fry for 1–2 minutes. Sprinkle over the sesame oil and green spring onion, and serve.

FIERY VEGETABLES IN COCONUT MILK

EIGHT CHILLIES MAY SEEM A BIT EXCESSIVE, ESPECIALLY IF YOU CHOOSE A SUPER-HOT VARIETY SUCH AS BIRD'S EYES, BUT REMEMBER THAT THE COCONUT MILK WILL PACIFY YOUR PALATE SOMEWHAT.

SERVES FOUR TO SIX

INGREDIENTS

450g/1lb mixed vegetables, such as aubergines (eggplant), baby sweetcorn, carrots, green beans, asparagus and patty pan squash
8 fresh red chillies, seeded
2 lemon grass stalks, tender portions chopped
4 kaffir lime leaves, torn
30ml/2 tbsp vegetable oil
250ml/8fl oz/1 cup coconut milk
30ml/2 tbsp Thai fish sauce (*nam pla*)
salt (optional)
15–20 fresh holy basil leaves, to garnish

COOK'S TIP

If you are unsure about the heat, use fewer chillies or mix hot with mild Anaheims or sweet (bell) peppers.

1 Trim the vegetables, then, using a sharp knife, cut them into pieces. They should all be more or less the same shape and thickness. Set aside.

2 Chop the fresh red chillies roughly and put them in a mortar. Add the lemon grass and kaffir lime leaves and grind to a paste. This can be done using a small blender, if you have one, or in the small bowl attachment of a food processor.

3 Heat the oil in a wok or large deep frying pan. Add the chilli mixture and fry over a medium heat for 2–3 minutes, stirring continuously.

4 Stir in the coconut milk and bring to the boil. Add the vegetables and cook for about 5 minutes or until they are all crisp-tender. Season with the fish sauce, and salt if needed. Spoon on to heated plates, garnish with holy basil leaves, and serve.

RED HOT CAULIFLOWER

VEGETABLES ARE SELDOM SERVED PLAIN IN MEXICO. THE CAULIFLOWER HERE IS FLAVOURED WITH A SIMPLE SERRANO AND TOMATO SALSA AND FRESH CHEESE.

SERVES SIX

INGREDIENTS
  1 small onion
  1 lime
  1 medium cauliflower
  400g/14oz can chopped tomatoes
  4 fresh serrano chillies, seeded and
    finely chopped
  1.5ml/¼ tsp granulated sugar
  75g/3oz feta cheese, crumbled
  salt
  chopped fresh flat leaf parsley,
    to garnish

1 Chop the onion very finely and place in a bowl. With a zester or sharp knife, peel away the zest of the lime in thin strips. Add the lime zest to the finely chopped onion.

2 Cut the lime in half and use a reamer or citrus squeezer to extract the juice from each half in turn, adding it to the onion and lime zest mixture. Set aside for the lime juice to soften the onion.

COOK'S TIP
A zester enables you to pare off tiny strips of lime rind with no pith.

3 Cut the cauliflower into florets. Tip the tomatoes into a pan and add the chillies and sugar. Heat gently. Meanwhile, bring a pan of water to the boil, add the cauliflower florets and cook gently for 5–8 minutes until tender.

4 Add the chopped onion mixture to the tomato salsa, with salt to taste. Stir and heat through, then spoon about one-third of the salsa into a serving dish.

5 Arrange the drained cauliflower florets on top of the salsa and spoon the remaining salsa on top.

6 Sprinkle with the feta, which should soften a little on contact. Serve immediately, sprinkled with chopped fresh flat leaf parsley.

MUSHROOMS WITH CHIPOTLE CHILLIES

CHIPOTLE CHILLIES ARE JALAPEÑOS THAT HAVE BEEN SMOKE-DRIED. THEIR SMOKY FLAVOUR IS THE PERFECT FOIL FOR THE MUSHROOMS IN THIS SIMPLE SALAD.

SERVES SIX

INGREDIENTS
    2 chipotle chillies
    450g/1lb/6 cups button
      (white) mushrooms
    60ml/4 tbsp vegetable oil
    1 onion, finely chopped
    2 garlic cloves, crushed or chopped
    salt
    small bunch of fresh coriander
      (cilantro), to garnish

VARIATION
Use cascabel instead of chipotle chillies. The name "cascabel" means "little rattle" and accurately describes the sound they make when shaken. Cascabel's nutty flavour is best appreciated when the skin is removed. Soak as for chipotle chillies, scoop out the flesh and add it to the onion and garlic.

1 Put the dried chillies in a heatproof bowl and pour over hot (not boiling) water to cover. Leave to stand for 20–30 minutes until they have softened. Drain, cut off the stalks, then slit the chillies and scrape out the seeds. Chop the flesh finely.

2 Trim the mushrooms, then clean them with a damp cloth or kitchen paper. If they are large, cut them in half.

3 Heat the oil in a large frying pan. Add the onion, garlic, chillies and mushrooms, and stir until evenly coated in the oil. Fry for 6–8 minutes, stirring occasionally, until the onion and mushrooms are tender.

4 Season with salt and spoon into a serving dish. Chop some of the coriander, leaving some whole leaves, and use to garnish. Serve hot.

CHEESE COURGETTES WITH GREEN CHILLIES

THIS IS A VERY TASTY WAY TO SERVE COURGETTES, WHICH CAN TASTE A BIT BLAND, AND THE DISH LOOKS GOOD TOO. SERVE IT AS A VEGETARIAN MAIN DISH OR AN UNUSUAL SIDE DISH.

2 Cut a cross in the base of each tomato. Place in a heatproof bowl and pour over boiling water to cover. Leave in the water for 30 seconds then lift out on a slotted spoon and plunge into a bowl of cold water. Drain. The skins will have begun to peel back from the crosses. Remove the skins, cut the tomatoes in half and squeeze out the seeds. Chop the flesh into strips.

3 Trim the courgettes, then cut them lengthways into 1cm/½in wide strips. Slice the strips into matchsticks.

4 Stir the courgettes into the onion mixture and fry for 10 minutes, stirring occasionally, until just tender. Add the tomatoes and chopped jalapeños, and cook for 2–3 minutes more.

5 Add the cream cheese. Reduce the heat to the lowest setting. As the cheese melts, stir gently to coat the courgettes. Season with salt, pile into a heated dish and serve, garnished with oregano. If serving as a main dish, warm, crusty, bread makes a good accompaniment. Alternatively, serve with boiled rice, or mixed into chunky pasta.

SERVES SIX

INGREDIENTS
- 30ml/2 tbsp vegetable oil
- ½ onion, thinly sliced
- 2 garlic cloves, crushed
- 5ml/1 tsp dried oregano
- 2 tomatoes
- 500g/1¼lb courgettes (zucchini)
- 50g/2oz/⅓ cup drained pickled jalapeño chilli slices, chopped
- 115g/4oz/½ cup cream cheese, cubed
- salt
- fresh oregano sprigs, to garnish

1 Heat the oil in a frying pan. Add the onion, garlic and dried oregano. Fry over gentle heat for 3–4 minutes, stirring frequently, until the onion is soft and translucent.

POTATOES WITH RED CHILLIES

IF YOU LIKE CHILLIES, YOU'LL LOVE THESE POTATOES! THE RED CHILLIES ADD COLOUR, FLAVOUR AND FIRE TO THE FINISHED DISH, WHICH IS FRAGRANCED WITH WARMING SPICES.

SERVES FOUR

INGREDIENTS

12–14 small new or salad
  potatoes, halved
30ml/2 tbsp vegetable oil
2.5ml/½ tsp crushed dried
  red chillies
2.5ml/½ tsp white cumin seeds
2.5ml/½ tsp fennel seeds
2.5ml/½ tsp crushed coriander seeds
5ml/1 tsp salt
1 onion, sliced
1–4 fresh red chillies, chopped
45ml/3 tbsp chopped fresh
  coriander (cilantro)

COOK'S TIP
After draining the cooked potatoes, cover
with kitchen paper and put on the lid.
The paper will absorb the steam and
leave the potatoes dry.

1 Bring a pan of lightly salted water to
the boil and cook the potatoes for about
15 minutes until tender but still firm.
Remove from the heat and drain off the
water. Set aside until needed.

2 Heat the oil in a deep frying pan and
add the crushed chillies, cumin, fennel
and coriander seeds. Sprinkle the salt
over and fry, stirring continuously, for
30–40 seconds.

3 Add the sliced onion and fry until
golden brown. Tip in the dry potatoes,
add the chopped red chillies and 15ml/
1 tbsp of the chopped coriander and
stir well.

4 Reduce the heat to very low, then
cover and cook for 5–7 minutes. Serve
the potatoes hot, on a heated dish,
garnished with the remaining chopped
fresh coriander.

SPICY ROOT VEGETABLE GRATIN

SUBTLY SPICED WITH CURRY POWDER, TURMERIC, CORIANDER AND MILD CHILLI POWDER, THIS RICH GRATIN IS SUBSTANTIAL ENOUGH TO SERVE ON ITS OWN.

2 Preheat the oven to 180°C/350°F/Gas 4. Heat half the butter in a heavy pan, and add the curry powder, turmeric and coriander. Stir in half the chilli powder. Cook for 2 minutes, then put aside to cool slightly.

3 Drain the vegetable slices, then pat them dry with kitchen paper. Place in a bowl, add the spice mixture and the shallots, and mix well.

SERVES FOUR

INGREDIENTS
  2 large potatoes, total weight
    about 450g/1lb
  2 sweet potatoes, total weight
    about 275g/10oz
  175g/6oz celeriac
  15ml/1 tbsp unsalted
    (sweet) butter
  5ml/1 tsp curry powder
  5ml/1 tsp ground turmeric
  2.5ml/½ tsp ground coriander
  5ml/1 tsp mild chilli powder
  3 shallots, chopped
  150ml/¼ pint/⅔ cup single
    (light) cream
  150ml/¼ pint/⅔ cup milk
  salt and ground black pepper
  chopped fresh flat leaf parsley,
    to garnish

1 Thinly slice the potatoes, sweet potatoes and celeriac, using a sharp knife or the slicing attachment in a food processor. Immediately place the slices in a bowl of cold water to prevent discolouring. Set aside.

VARIATION
Substitute parsnips or carrots for the sweet potatoes, and turnips for the celeriac.

4 Arrange the vegetables in a gratin dish, adding salt and pepper to each layer. Mix together the cream and milk, pour the mixture over the vegetables, then sprinkle the remaining chilli powder on top.

5 Cover with baking parchment and bake for about 45 minutes. Remove the parchment, dot with the remaining butter and bake for 50 minutes more until the top is golden. Serve garnished with the chopped fresh parsley.

COOK'S TIP
A salad of mixed leaves could be served separately with the gratin then some fresh fruit, such as mango, to follow.

LITTLE ONIONS COOKED WITH CHILLIES

WHOLE DRIED CHILLIES GIVE THIS SIMPLE DISH AN UNDERLYING WARMTH THAT ADDS TO ITS APPEAL.
FOR A SMOKY FLAVOUR, USE CHIPOTLE CHILLIES, OR AN ANAHEIM RED CHILLI.

SERVES SIX

INGREDIENTS
105ml/7 tbsp olive oil
675g/1½lb small onions
150ml/¼ pint/⅔ cup dry white wine
2 bay leaves
2 garlic cloves, bruised
1–2 small dried red chillies
15ml/1 tbsp coriander seeds, toasted
   and lightly crushed
2.5ml/½ tsp granulated sugar
a few fresh thyme sprigs
30ml/2 tbsp currants
10ml/2 tsp chopped fresh oregano
5ml/1 tsp grated (shredded)
   lemon rind
15ml/1 tbsp chopped fresh flat
   leaf parsley
30–45ml/2–3 tbsp pine nuts, toasted
salt and ground black pepper

1 Spoon 30ml/2 tbsp of the olive oil into a wide pan. Add the onions, place the pan over a medium heat and cook gently for about 5 minutes, or until the onions begin to colour. Use a slotted spoon to remove the onions from the pan and set them aside.

2 Add the remaining oil to the pan, with the wine, bay leaves, garlic, chillies, coriander seeds, sugar and thyme. Bring to the boil and cook for 5 minutes.

3 Return the onions to the pan. Add the currants, reduce the heat and cook gently for 15–20 minutes, or until the onions are tender but not falling apart. Use a slotted spoon to transfer the onions to a serving dish.

4 Boil the liquid vigorously until it reduces considerably. Taste and adjust the seasoning, if necessary, then pour it over the onions. Sprinkle the chopped fresh oregano over the cooked onions, cool, cover and then chill them for several hours.

VARIATION
The same method can be used for courgettes (zucchini), celery, small mushrooms, fennel and baby leeks. Cut the larger vegetables in 2.5cm/1in pieces and cook as for small onions.

5 Just before serving, stir in the grated lemon rind, chopped parsley and toasted pine nuts.

COOK'S TIPS
• Serve this dish as part of a mixed hors d'oeuvre – an antipasto – perhaps with a mild mayonnaise-dressed celeriac salad and some thinly sliced prosciutto or other air-dried ham.
• The aim of an hors d'oeuvre is to provide something beautifully fresh-looking that will arouse your appetite. Each dish should have its own taste.

Don't chill your chilli dishes, but do try them at room temperature. Spicy salads, especially those based on root vegetables, taste great with cold meat and poultry, and can also be served solo, with rustic bread or polenta. For main meal options, sample Chicken, Vegetable and Chilli Salad or Beef and Sweet Potato Salad with Mild Chilli Dressing.

Salads

HOT HOT CAJUN POTATO SALAD

IN CAJUN COUNTRY, WHERE TABASCO ORIGINATES, HOT MEANS REALLY HOT, SO YOU CAN GO TO TOWN WITH THIS SALAD IF YOU THINK YOU CAN TAKE IT!

SERVES SIX TO EIGHT

INGREDIENTS

    8 waxy potatoes
    1 green (bell) pepper, seeded
      and diced
    1 large gherkin, chopped
    4 spring onions (scallions), shredded
    3 eggs, hard-boiled (hard-cooked),
      shelled and chopped
    250ml/8fl oz/1 cup mayonnaise
    15ml/1 tbsp Dijon mustard
    Tabasco sauce, to taste
    pinch or 2 of cayenne
    salt and ground black pepper
    fanned, sliced gherkin, to garnish
    salad leaves, to serve

1 Put the unpeeled potatoes in a pan of cold salted water, bring to the boil and cook for 20–30 minutes, until tender. Drain. When the potatoes are cool enough to handle, peel them and cut into large chunks.

2 Place the potatoes in a large bowl and add the green pepper, gherkin, spring onions and eggs. Mix gently.

3 In a separate bowl, mix the mayonnaise with the mustard and season with salt, black pepper and Tabasco sauce to taste.

4 Add the dressing to the potato mixture, toss gently to coat, then sprinkle a pinch or 2 of cayenne on top. Garnish with fanned, sliced gherkin.

COOK'S TIP
To hard-boil eggs, pierce the round end so air can escape to prevent cracking. Place in boiling water for 8 minutes. Remove into cold water, then peel.

SALAD OF ROASTED SHALLOTS, CHILLIES AND BUTTERNUT SQUASH WITH FETA

THIS IS ESPECIALLY GOOD SERVED WITH A SALAD BASED ON RICE OR COUSCOUS. SERVE THE DISH WITH PLENTY OF GOOD, WARM, CRUSTY BREAD.

SERVES FOUR TO SIX

INGREDIENTS
75ml/5 tbsp olive oil
15ml/1 tbsp balsamic vinegar, plus
   a little extra if needed
15ml/1 tbsp sweet soy sauce
350g/12oz shallots, peeled but
   left whole
3 fresh red chillies
1 butternut squash, peeled, seeded
   and cut into chunks
5ml/1 tsp finely chopped fresh thyme
60ml/4 tbsp chopped fresh flat
   leaf parsley
1 small garlic clove, finely chopped
75g/3oz/¾ cup walnuts or pecan
   nuts, chopped
150g/5oz feta cheese
salt and ground black pepper

1 Preheat the oven to 200°C/400°F/
Gas 6. Beat the oil, vinegar and soy
sauce together in a large bowl.

2 Toss the shallots and 2 of the chillies
in the oil mixture and turn into a large,
shallow roasting pan or ovenproof dish.
Season with salt and pepper. Roast,
uncovered, for 25 minutes, stirring once
or twice.

3 Add the butternut squash and roast
for a further 35–40 minutes, stirring
once, until the squash is tender and
browned. Remove from the oven, stir
in the chopped thyme and set the
vegetable mixture aside to cool.

4 Mix the parsley and garlic together
and stir in the nuts. Seed and finely
chop the remaining chilli.

5 Stir the parsley, garlic and nut mixture
into the cooled vegetables. Add chopped
chilli to taste and adjust the seasoning,
adding a little extra balsamic vinegar if
you like. Crumble the feta cheese and
add it to the salad, tossing together
lightly. Transfer to a serving dish and
serve immediately, at room temperature
rather than chilled.

SWEET POTATO, PEPPER AND CHILLI SALAD

THIS SALAD IS COMPOSED OF A DELICIOUS BLEND OF INGREDIENTS AND HAS A TRULY TROPICAL TASTE. IT IS IDEAL SERVED WITH ASIAN OR CARIBBEAN DISHES.

2 Meanwhile, mix the dressing ingredients together in a bowl and season to taste.

3 Put the red pepper in a large bowl and add the celery and onion. Tip in the finely chopped chilli and mix with a wooden spoon.

4 Remove the sweet potatoes from the oven. When they are cool enough to handle, peel them. Cut them into cubes and add them to the large bowl. Drizzle the dressing over and toss carefully. Season again to taste and serve, garnished with fresh coriander.

VARIATION
This would work well with potatoes.

SERVES FOUR TO SIX

INGREDIENTS
　　1kg/2¼lb sweet potatoes
　　1 red (bell) pepper, seeded and
　　　finely diced
　　3 celery sticks, finely diced
　　¼ red skinned onion, finely chopped
　　1 fresh red chilli, finely chopped
　　salt and ground black pepper
For the dressing
　　45ml/3 tbsp chopped fresh coriander
　　　(cilantro), plus extra to garnish
　　juice of 1 lime
　　150ml/¼ pint/⅔ cup natural
　　　(plain) yogurt

1 Preheat the oven to 200°C/400°F/ Gas 6. Wash the potatoes and pat dry with kitchen paper, pierce them all over and bake in the oven for 40 minutes or until tender.

GREEN PAPAYA <u>AND</u> CHILLI SALAD

THIS SALAD APPEARS IN MANY GUISES IN SOUTH~EAST ASIA. AS GREEN PAPAYA IS NOT EASY TO FIND, FINELY SHREDDED CARROTS, CUCUMBER OR GREEN APPLE CAN BE USED INSTEAD.

SERVES FOUR

INGREDIENTS

1 green papaya
4 garlic cloves, roughly chopped
15ml/1 tbsp chopped shallots
3–4 fresh red chillies, seeded and
  sliced, plus extra sliced fresh red
  chillies to garnish (optional)
2.5ml/½ tsp salt
2–3 snake beans or 6 green beans,
  cut into 2cm/¾ in lengths
2 tomatoes, cut into thin wedges
45ml/3 tbsp Thai fish sauce
  (*nam pla*)
15ml/1 tbsp granulated sugar
juice of 1 lime
30ml/2 tbsp crushed roasted peanuts

3 Add the sliced beans and wedges of tomato to the mortar and crush them lightly with the pestle.

VARIATION
Use cashew nuts instead of peanuts.

4 Flavour the mixture with the fish sauce, sugar and lime juice – you will not need extra salt. Transfer the salad to a serving dish and sprinkle with crushed peanuts. Garnish with the extra sliced red chillies, if using, and serve.

1 Cut the papaya in half lengthways. Scrape out the seeds with a spoon, then peel, using a swivel vegetable peeler or a small sharp knife. Shred the flesh finely using a food processor or grater.

2 Put the garlic, shallots, sliced chillies and salt in a large mortar and grind to a paste with a pestle. Add the shredded papaya, a little at a time, pounding until it becomes slightly limp and soft.

ROASTED PEPPER AND TOMATO SALAD

CHILLIES DO NOT NEED TO DOMINATE TO MAKE THEIR PRESENCE FELT IN A DISH. HERE THEY ARE USED TO ACCENTUATE THE FLAVOUR OF THEIR MILDER RELATIONS, THE SWEET PEPPERS.

SERVES FOUR

INGREDIENTS

3 red (bell) peppers
6 large plum tomatoes
2.5ml/½ tsp dried red chilli flakes
1 red onion, finely sliced
3 garlic cloves, finely chopped
grated rind and juice of 1 lemon
45ml/3 tbsp chopped fresh flat
  leaf parsley
30ml/2 tbsp extra virgin olive oil
  or chilli oil
salt
black and green olives and extra
  chopped flat leaf parsley, to garnish

COOK'S TIPS
• Peppers roasted this way will keep for several weeks. After peeling off the skins, place the pepper pieces in a jar with a tight-fitting lid. Pour over olive oil to cover. Store in the refrigerator.
• For an intense flavour, roast fresh red chillies with the peppers and tomatoes.

1 Preheat the oven to 220°C/425°F/ Gas 7. Place the peppers on a baking tray and roast, turning occasionally, for 10 minutes or until the skins are almost blackened. Add the tomatoes to the baking tray, return to the oven and roast for 5 minutes more.

2 Place the roasted peppers in a plastic bag, close the top loosely, trapping in the steam to loosen the skins, and then set them aside, with the tomatoes, until they are cool enough to handle, which should take about 15 minutes.

3 Carefully pull off the skin from the peppers. Remove the seeds, then chop the peppers and tomatoes roughly and place in a mixing bowl.

4 Add the chilli flakes, onion slices, chopped garlic, lemon rind and juice. Sprinkle over the parsley. Mix well, then transfer to a serving dish.

5 Sprinkle with a little salt, drizzle over the olive oil or chilli oil and sprinkle olives and extra parsley over the top. Serve at room temperature.

SPINACH AND SERRANO CHILLI SALAD

YOUNG SPINACH LEAVES MAKE A WELCOME CHANGE FROM LETTUCE AND ARE EXCELLENT IN SALADS.
THE ROASTED GARLIC IS AN INSPIRED ADDITION TO THE DRESSING.

SERVES SIX

INGREDIENTS

   500g/1¼lb baby spinach leaves
   50g/2oz/⅓ cup sesame seeds
   50g/2oz/¼ cup butter
   30ml/2 tbsp olive oil
   6 shallots, sliced
   8 fresh serrano chillies, seeded and
     cut into strips
   4 tomatoes, sliced
For the dressing
   6 smoked or roasted garlic cloves
   120ml/4fl oz/½ cup white
     wine vinegar
   2.5ml/½ tsp ground white pepper
   1 bay leaf
   2.5ml/½ tsp ground allspice
   30ml/2 tbsp chopped fresh thyme,
     plus extra sprigs, to garnish

1 Pull any coarse stalks from the spinach leaves, rinse the leaves and dry them in a salad spinner or clean dishtowel. Put them in a plastic bag in the refrigerator.

2 Make the dressing. Remove the skins from the garlic, then chop the flesh and put it in a jar that has a screw-top lid. Add the vinegar, pepper, bay leaf, allspice and chopped thyme. Close tightly, shake well, then set aside.

COOK'S TIP
You can buy smoked garlic from most supermarkets. If you prefer to use roasted garlic, place the cloves in a roasting pan in an oven preheated to 180°C/350°F/Gas 4 and cook for about 15 minutes until soft.

3 Toast the sesame seeds in a dry frying pan, shaking frequently over a medium heat until golden. Set aside.

4 Heat the butter and oil in a frying pan. Fry the shallots for 4–5 minutes, until softened, then stir in the chilli strips and fry for 2–3 minutes more.

5 In a large bowl, layer the spinach with the shallot and chilli mixture, and the tomato slices. Pour over the dressing. Sprinkle with sesame seeds and serve, garnished with thyme sprigs.

VARIATION
For a crunchy salad, use finely sliced red or white cabbage instead of spinach.

CHICKEN, VEGETABLE AND CHILLI SALAD

THIS VIETNAMESE SALAD IS FULL OF SURPRISING TEXTURES AND FLAVOURS. SERVE AS A LIGHT LUNCH DISH OR FOR SUPPER WITH CRUSTY FRENCH BREAD.

SERVES FOUR

INGREDIENTS
225g/8oz Chinese leaves
(Chinese cabbage)
2 carrots, cut in matchsticks
½ cucumber, cut in matchsticks
2 fresh red chillies, seeded and cut
into thin strips
1 small onion, sliced into fine rings
4 pickled gherkins, sliced into fine
rings, plus 45ml/3 tbsp of the
liquid from the jar
50g/2oz/½ cup peanuts, lightly ground
225g/8oz cooked chicken, sliced
1 garlic clove, crushed
5ml/1 tsp granulated sugar
30ml/2 tbsp cider or white
wine vinegar
salt

COOK'S TIP
Add extra cider or white wine vinegar to
the dressing for a sharper taste.

1 Discard any tough, outer leaves from
the Chinese leaves, then stack the
remainder on a board. Using a sharp
knife, cut them into shreds that are
about the same width as the carrot
matchsticks. Put the Chinese leaves
and carrot matchsticks in a salad bowl.

2 Spread out the cucumber matchsticks
in a colander and sprinkle with salt.
Stand the colander on a plate and set
aside for 15 minutes, to extract the
excess liquid.

3 Mix the chillies and onion rings in a
small bowl. Add the sliced gherkins and
peanuts. Rinse the salted cucumber
thoroughly, drain well and pat dry with
kitchen paper.

4 Add the cucumber matchsticks to
the salad bowl and toss together lightly.
Stir in the chilli mixture. Arrange the
chicken on top. In a bowl, whisk the
gherkin liquid with the garlic, sugar and
vinegar. Pour over the salad, toss lightly
and serve.

BEEF AND SWEET POTATO SALAD WITH MILD CHILLI DRESSING

THIS SALAD MAKES A GOOD MAIN DISH FOR A SUMMER BUFFET. IT IS DELICIOUS WITH A SIMPLE POTATO SALAD AND SOME PEPPERY LEAVES.

SERVES SIX TO EIGHT

INGREDIENTS
   800g/1¾lb fillet (tenderloin) of beef
   15ml/1 tbsp black peppercorns,
    lightly crushed
   10ml/2 tsp chopped fresh thyme
   60ml/4 tbsp olive oil
   450g/1lb orange-fleshed sweet
    potatoes, peeled
   salt and ground black pepper
For the dressing
   1 garlic clove, chopped
   60ml/4 tbsp fresh flat leaf parsley
   30ml/2 tbsp chopped fresh
    coriander (cilantro)
   15ml/1 tbsp small salted capers,
    rinsed and drained
   ½–1 fresh green chilli, seeded
    and chopped
   10ml/2 tsp Dijon mustard
   10–15ml/2–3 tsp white wine vinegar
   75ml/5 tbsp extra virgin olive oil
   2 shallots, finely chopped

1 Roll the beef in the crushed peppercorns and thyme. Cover and set aside for 2–3 hours. Preheat the oven to 200°C/400°F/Gas 6.

2 Heat half the olive oil in a heavy frying pan. Add the beef and brown it all over, turning frequently, to seal it. Place in a roasting pan and cook in the oven for 15–20 minutes.

COOK'S TIP
Choose a mild chilli such as Italia, if you can locate it. An Anaheim would also be good, but peel before chopping.

3 Remove the beef from the oven, cover with foil, allow to rest for 10–15 minutes.

4 Meanwhile, preheat the grill (broiler). Cut the sweet potatoes into 1cm/½in slices. Brush with the remaining olive oil, season to taste with salt and pepper, and grill (broil) for about 5–6 minutes on each side, until tender and browned. Cut the sweet potato slices into strips and place them in a bowl.

5 Cut the beef into slices or strips and toss with the sweet potato, then set the bowl aside.

6 Make the dressing. Put the garlic, parsley, coriander, capers, chilli, mustard and 10ml/2 tsp of the vinegar in a food processor or blender and process until chopped. With the motor still running, gradually pour in the oil to make a smooth dressing. Season with salt and pepper, and add more vinegar, to taste. Stir in the shallots.

7 Toss the dressing with the sweet potatoes and beef, and leave to stand for up to 2 hours before serving.

VARIATIONS
• Use pork or ham joints instead of beef.
• Try Bordeaux mustard instead of Dijon. It has a mild aromatic flavour.

SCALLOP CONCHIGLIE

SCALLOPS, PASTA AND ROCKET ARE FLAVOURED WITH ROASTED PEPPER, CHILLI AND BALSAMIC VINEGAR.

2 Make the vinaigrette. Put the vinegar in a bowl and stir in the honey until dissolved. Add the chopped pepper, chillies and garlic, then whisk in the oil.

3 Bring a large pan of lightly salted water to the boil and cook the pasta for 10–12 minutes, or until *al dente.*

4 Meanwhile, heat the oil and butter in a frying pan until sizzling. Add half the scallops and toss over a high heat for 2 minutes. Remove with a slotted spoon and keep warm. Cook the remaining scallops in the same way.

5 Add the wine to the liquid remaining in the pan and stir over a high heat until the mixture has reduced to a few tablespoons. Remove from the heat and keep warm.

SERVES FOUR

INGREDIENTS
8 large fresh scallops
300g/11oz/2¾ cups dried conchiglie
  or other pasta shapes
15ml/1 tbsp olive oil
15g/½oz/1 tbsp butter
120ml/4fl oz/½ cup dry white wine
90g/3½oz/1½–2 cups rocket
  (arugula) leaves, stalks trimmed
salt and ground black pepper
For the vinaigrette
15ml/1 tbsp balsamic vinegar
5–10ml/1–2 tsp clear honey,
  to taste
1 piece bottled roasted (bell) pepper,
  drained and finely chopped
1–2 fresh red chillies, seeded
  and chopped
1 garlic clove, crushed
60ml/4 tbsp extra virgin olive oil

1 Unless the fishmonger has already done so, remove the dark beard-like fringe and tough muscle from the scallops. Cut each of the scallops into 2–3 pieces. If the corals are attached, pull them off and cut each piece in half. Season with salt and pepper.

VARIATION
Use prawns (shrimp) instead of scallops.

6 Drain the pasta and tip it into a warmed bowl. Add the rocket, scallops, the reduced cooking juices and the vinaigrette, and toss well to combine.

COOK'S TIP
This is best prepared using fresh scallops, which look creamy-grey. If pure white they will have been frozen.

SPICY SQUID SALAD

THIS TASTY, COLOURFUL SALAD IS A REFRESHING WAY OF SERVING SQUID. THE GINGER AND CHILLI DRESSING IS ADDED WHILE THE SQUID IS STILL HOT, AND FLAVOURS THE SHELLFISH AND BEANS.

SERVES FOUR

INGREDIENTS
   450g/1lb squid
   300ml/½ pint/1¼ cups fish stock
   175g/6oz green beans, trimmed
      and halved
   45ml/3 tbsp fresh coriander
      (cilantro) leaves
   10ml/2 tsp granulated sugar
   30ml/2 tbsp rice vinegar
   5ml/1 tsp sesame oil
   15ml/1 tbsp light soy sauce
   15ml/1 tbsp vegetable oil
   2 garlic cloves, finely chopped
   10ml/2 tbsp finely chopped fresh
      root ginger
   1 fresh chilli, seeded and chopped
   salt

3 Bring the fish stock to the boil in a wok or pan. Add all the squid pieces, then lower the heat and cook for about 2 minutes until they are tender and have curled. Drain.

4 Bring a pan of lightly salted water to the boil, add the beans and cook them for 3–5 minutes, until they are crisp-tender. Drain, refresh under cold water or turn into a bowl of iced water, then drain again. Mix the squid and beans in a serving bowl.

5 In a bowl, mix the coriander leaves, sugar, rice vinegar, sesame oil and soy sauce. Pour the mixture over the squid and beans, and toss lightly, using a spoon, to coat.

6 Heat the vegetable oil in a wok or small pan. When it is very hot, stir-fry the garlic, ginger and chilli for a few seconds, then pour the dressing over the squid mixture. Toss gently and leave for at least 5 minutes. Add salt to taste and serve warm or cold.

1 Prepare the squid. Holding the body in one hand, gently pull away the head and tentacles. Discard the head then trim and reserve the tentacles. Remove the transparent "quill" from inside the body of the squid and peel off the purplish skin on the outside.

2 Cut the body of the squid open lengthways and wash thoroughly. Score criss-cross patterns on the inside, taking care not to cut through the flesh completely, then cut into 7.5 × 5cm/ 3 × 2in pieces.

COOK'S TIPS
• If you hold your knife at an angle when scoring the squid, there is less of a risk of cutting right through it.
• Always make sure your knives are kept sharp to make cutting easier.

SPICY VEGETABLE RIBBONS

FEW SALADS LOOK PRETTIER THAN THIS COMBINATION OF CUCUMBER, CARROT AND MOOLI RIBBONS, TOSSED WITH BEANSPROUTS AND SPIKED WITH CHILLI.

2 Wash the beansprouts and drain them thoroughly in a colander. Pat them dry with kitchen paper.

3 Peel the cucumber, cut it in half lengthwise and scoop out and discard the seeds. Peel the cucumber flesh into long ribbon strips, using a swivel vegetable peeler or mandoline.

SERVES FOUR

INGREDIENTS
  225g/8oz/4 cups beansprouts
  1 cucumber
  2 carrots
  1 small mooli (daikon)
  1 small red onion, thinly sliced
  2.5cm/1in fresh root ginger, peeled
    and cut into thin matchsticks
  1 small fresh red chilli, seeded and
    thinly sliced
  handful of fresh coriander (cilantro)
    leaves or fresh mint leaves
For the dressing
  15ml/1 tbsp rice vinegar
  15ml/1 tbsp light soy sauce
  15ml/1 tbsp Thai fish sauce
    (*nam pla*)
  1 garlic clove, finely chopped
  15ml/1 tbsp sesame oil
  45ml/3 tbsp groundnut (peanut) oil
  30ml/2 tbsp sesame seeds,
    lightly toasted

1 First make the dressing by mixing all the ingredients in a bottle or screw-top jar and shaking vigorously.

COOK'S TIPS
• Keep beansprouts refrigerated and use within a day of purchase.
• Mooli, which looks like a white parsnip, has a fresh, peppery taste. Eat it raw or cooked, but as it has a high water content it needs to be salted before cooking.
• Refrigerated, the dressing will keep for a couple of days.

4 Peel the carrots and mooli into ribbons as for the cucumber.

5 Place the carrots, mooli and cucumber ribbons in a large shallow serving dish, add the beansprouts, onion, ginger, chilli and coriander or mint and toss to mix. Pour the dressing over the salad just before serving.

GADO-GADO <u>WITH</u> PEANUT <u>AND</u> CHILLI SAUCE

A BANANA LEAF, WHICH CAN BE BOUGHT FROM ASIAN FOOD STORES, CAN BE USED AS WELL AS THE MIXED SALAD LEAVES TO LINE THE PLATTER FOR A SPECIAL OCCASION.

SERVES SIX

INGREDIENTS
  ½ cucumber
  2 pears (not too ripe) or 175g/6oz
    wedge of yam bean (jicama)
  1–2 eating apples
  juice of ½ lemon
  mixed salad leaves
  6 small tomatoes, cut in wedges
  3 slices fresh pineapple, cored and
    cut in wedges
  3 eggs, hard-boiled (hard-cooked)
    and shelled
  175g/6oz egg noodles, cooked,
    cooled and chopped
  deep-fried onions, to garnish
For the peanut sauce
  2–4 fresh red chillies, seeded
    and ground, or 15ml/1 tbsp
    chilli sambal
  300ml/½ pint/1¼ cups coconut milk
  350g/12oz/1¼ cups crunchy
    peanut butter
  15ml/1 tbsp dark soy sauce or soft
    dark brown sugar
  5ml/1 tsp tamarind pulp, soaked in
    45ml/3 tbsp warm water
  coarsely crushed peanuts
  salt

1 Make the peanut sauce. Put the chillies or chilli sambal in a pan. Pour in the coconut milk. Stir in the peanut butter. Heat gently, stirring, until mixed.

COOK'S TIP
To make your own peanut butter, process roasted peanuts in a food processor, slowly adding vegetable oil to achieve the right texture. Add salt to taste.

2 Simmer gently until the sauce thickens, then stir in the soy sauce or sugar. Strain in the tamarind juice, add salt to taste and stir well. Spoon into a bowl and sprinkle with a few coarsely crushed peanuts.

VARIATION
Quail's eggs can be used instead of hen's eggs and look very attractive in this dish. Hard-boil for 3 minutes, shell, then halve or leave whole.

3 To make the salad, core the cucumber and peel the pears or yam bean. Cut them into matchsticks. Finely shred the apples and sprinkle them with the lemon juice. Spread a bed of salad leaves on a flat platter, then pile the fruit and vegetables on top.

4 Add the sliced or quartered hard-boiled eggs, the chopped noodles and the deep-fried onions. Serve at once, with the sauce.

INDEX